Contents

"We are limited only by our imagination."

— Arthur C. Clarke

1. Glimmering Through the Stars: Humanity's Cosmic Aspirations

Throughout the ages, humankind has gazed up at the stars with wonder, asking questions both profound and whimsical. We have mapped their movements, told stories about their origins, and even ventured a few gentle steps towards their bright complexity. But what if our loftiest ambitions were no longer tethered by the familiar confines of our planet and technology? What if our imagination scaffolded a bridge to living among the stars themselves?

The theoretical Dyson Sphere, a colossal structure capable of capturing the entirety of a star's energy output, ignites such dreams. While largely speculative, the mere notion of such an existence allows us to explore the boundaries of our potential, both scientifically and philosophically. In "Living with a Dyson Sphere," we embark on a detailed exploration of these hypothetical alien megastructures, their implications, and the possibilities they possess within the vast theater of the universe. Join me, Eileen Patricia Miller, as we unravel the strands of science, technology, and imagination to envision a life where the cosmos is no longer a distant spectator but an integral part of human existence.

2. The Birth of a Vision: Dyson's Dream

2.1. The Mind of Freeman Dyson

Freeman Dyson, a towering intellect of the 20th century, was not only a theoretical physicist but also a visionary whose thoughts traversed the borders of science and philosophy. Born in 1923 in Crowthorne, England, and later residing in the United States, Dyson's insatiable curiosity and innovative thinking ignited a firestorm of ideas surrounding the evolution of life and technology within the cosmos. His contributions have advanced our understanding of both fundamental physics and speculative astrophysics, most notably through the concept that bears his name—the Dyson Sphere.

Fascinated by the nature of stars and the potential for harnessing their immense energy, Dyson's mind was an intricate tapestry of scientific inquiry interwoven with imaginations of cosmic possibilities. His academic journey began with a stellar trajectory, earning a scholarship to the prestigious Royal College of Science, London, followed by a stint at the University of Cambridge. He pursued advanced studies in physics, participating in groundbreaking research during and after World War II. His time working on radar technology for the United Kingdom's wartime efforts molded his analytical skills, which would later enable him to explore the grander metaphysics of the universe.

The inception of the Dyson Sphere concept arose from a simple yet profound query: how would an advanced civilization capitalize on the energy output of its star? Dyson proposed that an advanced species would engineer a megastructure enveloping a star to collect as much energy as possible, effectively maximizing its power consumption. This radical idea was brought forth in 1960, laid out in his seminal paper, "Search for Artificial Stellar Sources of Infrared Radiation." In it, he posited that any civilization capable of such an engineering feat would inevitably generate immense heat detectable as infrared radiation—a notion that would later inspire the Search for Extraterrestrial Intelligence (SETI) movement.

Dyson's vision extended beyond mere energy collection; it questioned the very nature of our understanding of civilization and existence. His ability to synthesize ideas from various disciplines was rooted in a creatively scientific mindset. He seamlessly blended rigorous analytical thought with poetic reflections on human existence, a characteristic that set him apart from many of his contemporaries. He once remarked, "The great advances in science usually result from new techniques rather than new concepts." This philosophy underscores his belief that innovation arises not only from imaginative frameworks but also from the development of new tools and methodologies to explore the universe.

His mind was also shaped by a profound appreciation for the interconnectedness of life, technology, and the cosmos. He understood that the evolution of civilizations is inherently tied to their creative and technological undertakings. In Dyson's view, the ability to construct a megastructure like the Dyson Sphere symbolizes a leap in the evolutionary trajectory of humanity—a willingness to transcend limitations and redefine existence on a galactic scale. He envisioned such structures not merely as mechanical solutions to energy problems but as extensions of consciousness, representing humanity's relentless drive toward exploration and understanding.

Central to Dyson's speculation was the recognition of civilization in various forms, ranging from our own terrestrial existence to potential alien societies thriving among the stars. He initiated thought experiments about what an advanced civilization would look like and how it might function. His concept of a Dyson Sphere sought to envision a new paradigm within which life could flourish—one that transcends local constraints and embraces the bounteous energy and resources found in the cosmos.

Dyson's ideas sparked not only scientific discourse but also a multitude of philosophical inquiries about life in the universe. In his mind, the possibility of alien megastructures and extraterrestrial intelligence was not an abstract dream, but a tangible exploration of our place in the universal fabric. He often emphasized the ethical dimensions of our technological ambitions, pondering how the pursuit of mega-engineering might reflect humanity's values and aspirations.

Moreover, Dyson's legacy extends to how we engage with the universe on both a scientific and cultural level. He fostered conversations about the implications of vast technological undertakings, urging society to ponder the consequences of engineering at such grand scales. The conversations he initiated resonate with contemporary discussions around sustainability and the ethical responsibilities that accompany advanced technologies.

As we delve deeper into a future where Dyson's vision may become reality, we are continually reminded of his axiomatic belief in the necessity of bold thought: "We are not only going to the stars; we are becoming the stars." This reflection urges us to consider not just the tangible constructs we may build or the energy we may harness, but the vision of humanity that evolves through such endeavors.

Understanding the mind of Freeman Dyson opens doors to a multitude of perspectives regarding life and technology beyond our planet. His pioneering spirit and audacious thinking are vital as we contemplate the future of our existence and the high potential embodied in concepts like the Dyson Sphere. Drawing from Dyson's comprehensive vision, we embark on a journey toward realizing the possibilities of cosmic dwelling, an endeavor that may one day challenge the very essence of what it means to be human in a boundless universe.

2.2. Early Concepts of Megastructures

The journey towards conceptualizing megastructures is deeply entwined with the evolution of human thought, marked by curiosity, ambition, and the desire to transcend limitations. As the fascination with the cosmos grew over the centuries, so too did the ideas regarding large-scale constructs that could harness and manipulate the energies of celestial bodies. Early concepts of these megastructures can be traced back to the foundations laid by astronomers, philosophers, and science fiction writers who sought to expand the boundaries of human understanding and capability.

Ancient civilizations often looked to the heavens in wonder, creating myths and stories that reflected their knowledge of astronomy and their desire to connect with the celestial. Structures like the Pyramids of Giza, while not megastructures in the modern sense, symbolize humanity's ambition to create monumental works that mirror the grandeur of the stars. The shape of the pyramids itself—pointing upwards—can be seen as an early representation of humanity's aspirations, as if reaching toward the divine or the cosmic unknown.

The philosophical inquiries of the ancients also contributed to this evolution. Figures such as Plato and Aristotle speculated on the nature of the cosmos, presenting ideas of celestial spheres and a structured universe that hinted at the possibility of manipulating heavenly forces. This cosmic imagination laid a groundwork that would eventually inspire thoughts on energy collection and usage at a grand scale. However, it was not until the Renaissance, with its revival of scientific inquiry, that the seeds for modern megastructure theory were firmly planted.

The scientific revolution sparked new ways of thinking about and interacting with the cosmos. Figures like Johannes Kepler and Galileo Galilei championed ideas about the structure and mechanics of the universe that began to set the stage for engineering concepts beyond Earth. Kepler's laws of planetary motion, particularly, reflected the possibility of understanding celestial mechanics to a degree where one could conceive of constructing structures within that framework. It was this era that saw the first inklings of space travel fantasies, albeit largely theoretical, culminating in visions of humanity's potential to climb beyond the confines of its own planet.

As the 20th century dawned, the landscape of thought around megastructures began to take a more tangible form. With the advent of modern physics, particularly Einstein's theories of relativity, the scientific community was equipped with the tools needed to think beyond traditional mass and energy paradigms. This period also witnessed a blossoming of science fiction as a genre that powerfully influenced the imagination regarding the possibilities of advanced engineering. Authors like Isaac Asimov and Arthur C. Clarke not only speculated on the nature of future technologies but often touched upon concepts akin to megastructures in their storytelling. Clarke's concept of the space elevator and the infrastructure necessary for interstellar travel hinted at the ambitious engineering feats humanity might one day accomplish.

The first explicit theoretical framework for megastructures resembling the Dyson Sphere emerged in the latter half of the 20th century, primarily through the work of Freeman Dyson. However, Dyson's groundbreaking proposal can be seen as part of a continuum of ideas, influenced by earlier thinkers and imagined futures. His vision was radical, suggesting a structure that would capture the energy output of an entire star, but it was also a logical extension of existing theories about energy, technology, and civilization itself.

Moreover, the idea of using the cosmos to support life and civilization can be traced back through various conceptualizations of large-scale energy management and habitation. Concepts like O'Neill cylinders, proposed by physicist Gerard K. O'Neill, exemplified early thoughts on creating habitable spaces in orbit. These ideas effectively bridged the gap between theoretical constructs and practical engineering challenges, highlighting a growing awareness of the need for sustainable energy sources to support expanding human endeavors in space.

In the context of Dyson's original proposal, the megastructure embodies the ambition to not only survive but thrive on a cosmic scale. By envisioning an energy-harvesting sphere around a star, Dyson catalyzed discussions about the potential for civilizations to evolve in ways that transcend the current human experience. He encouraged thinking about the medium through which civilizations interact with their environment, examining how such structures could enable expansive growth and exploration.

Critically, early concepts of megastructures weren't free of philosophical implications. They symbolized humanity's relentless quest for knowledge and mastery over nature, which carries with it ethical questions about the consequences of such ambitions. The civilizations capable of constructing Dyson Spheres would not just be those adept at engineering but also those capable of navigating the ethical dimensions of their power. Early thinkers grappled with the responsibilities that accompany such mastery, positing that greatness must also consider the broader impacts of such construction on local and universal ecosystems.

Thus, early concepts of megastructures serve as a reflection of humanity's deep-seated aspirations and the challenges that come from pursuing the limits of our understanding. They tie together strands of philosophy, ethics, science fiction, and speculative engineering, illustrating a timeless quest to intertwine existence with the cosmos' vast energies. As we continue our exploration of specific megastructures like the Dyson Sphere, we remain grounded in this rich historical narrative, drawing inspiration from the intellectual foundations laid by those who dared to imagine a future unfettered by the limitations of the past.

2.3. A Visionary's Proposal

Freeman Dyson's groundbreaking concept of a star-encompassing structure is rooted in the interplay of several key ideas that together illuminate why he believed such an ambitious undertaking was both possible and imperative for an advanced civilization. At its core, the proposal of a Dyson Sphere responds to the fundamental question of energy management facing any celestial society. By capturing the vast energy output of a star, a Dyson Sphere not only addresses the immediate energy concerns of a civilization but also paves the way for exponential growth and expansion. Dyson's vision resonates with the timeless human aspiration to overcome limitations—not just in terms of energy consumption but also in our capacity for exploration, creativity, and development.

To understand the logic behind Dyson's proposal, one must first appreciate the sheer scale of stellar energy output. Our sun, a relatively average star, emits energy equivalent to approximately 386 billion billion watts per second. This staggering figure illustrates the limitless potential available to any civilization capable of harnessing it. The need for vast energy sources becomes progressively more pressing as civilizations evolve, with demands escalating in tandem with technological advancement. Dyson proposed that a civilization that reaches the technology maturity required for interstellar aspirations would soon find its current energy sources insufficient. Harnessing a star's energy would not merely supplement a civilization's needs; it would redefine its possible futures.

Dyson's thoughts were heavily influenced by the laws of thermodynamics and the efficiency limits that govern energy utilization. He envisioned the Dyson Sphere as a way to maximize energy absorption while mitigating losses. Traditional energy collection on planetary surfaces, such as solar panels, inherently suffers from geographic and atmospheric limitations. In contrast, a Dyson Sphere, by directly surrounding a star, could theoretically capture a far greater percentage of solar energy with minimal loss due to distance or obstruction.

Dyson did not stop at proposing a simple spherical structure. His ideas branched out into possibilities for what would later be categorized as different variants of Dyson Spheres, such as Dyson swarms or Dyson bubbles. Each variant holds unique attributes and challenges, all rooted in the fundamental principle of optimizing energy collection while ensuring structural integrity. These constructs, no matter their form, underscore Dyson's belief that innovation is necessary not only in engineering but also in the philosophical mindset regarding our interaction with energy and its uses.

The implications of Dyson's vision extend far beyond mere energy acquisition. The construction of a Dyson Sphere gestures toward a broader societal evolution—a civilization that constructs such a structure would likely need to reimagine its social contracts, technological landscapes, and philosophical orientations. Dyson anticipated that the pursuit of constructing a sphere or swarm around a star would yield transformational breakthroughs in technologies associated with materials science, robotics, artificial intelligence, and energy transmission. Each aspect of such an endeavor necessitates advancements in multiple fields, showcasing the interconnectedness of scientific disciplines.

Moreover, the capacity to harness a star's energy reflections upon civilization's ethical responsibilities. While humanity has often sought to manipulate the natural world for progress, Dyson's proposal illustrates a pivotal moment where that manipulation becomes cosmic in scale. What responsibilities come with wielding such extraordinary power over energy resources? A society capable of building a Dyson Sphere would face complex ethical dilemmas surrounding resource management, environmental stewardship, and the interaction with potential extraterrestrial intelligences within the cosmic expanse.

Dyson envisioned the Dyson Sphere as a manifestation of what humanity's aspirations could culminate in: a structure that epitomizes our desire not only for survival but for thriving within the universe's vast expanses. His proposal urges us to look beyond our terrestrial confines and consider a future where the stars are not distant objects of admiration but intertwined with the fabric of our existence. This osmotic relationship with the cosmos could spark new philosophical inquiries, challenging our understanding of what it means to be a civilization among the stars.

In essence, Dyson's visionary proposal is a bold synthesis of scientific possibility, technological ambition, and profound philosophical inquiry. As we consider the ramifications of such mega-engineering projects, it becomes clear that the conversation surrounding Dyson Sphere-like constructs carries weight far beyond technical feasibility; it encompasses the entirety of human potential. His work invariably nudges us to contemplate not just the mechanics of constructing such structures but also the essence of what drives civilizations towards greatness. It serves as a clarion call for humanity to act courageously —dream boldly, build patiently, and reflect deeply—as we stand poised to engage with the cosmos in unprecedented ways.

2.4. Reception and Impact

Freeman Dyson's proposal for the vast and ambitious Dyson Sphere did not emerge into a vacuum; it entered a scientific and cultural milieu ripe for exploration yet firmly grounded in skepticism and cautious curiosity. Initial reactions to Dyson's theories in the scientific community ranged from intrigue to skepticism, embodying a typical phase in the reception of revolutionary ideas. In 1960, when Dyson first introduced his concept in a paper titled "Search for Artificial Stellar Sources of Infrared Radiation," he sparked a firestorm of interest, not just among physicists and engineers, but also among science fiction enthusiasts and futurists, echoing widespread speculation about the future of civilization.

The community's response included a blend of fascination and disbelief. Many scientists found the technical aspects of the Dyson Sphere stimulating, seeing it as a new frontier in energy utilization and astrophysical engineering. Those captivated by Dyson's insights began to consider what this meant for the evolution of civilization. The implications of a theoretically realizable structure capable of harnessing the energy output of an entire star led to groundbreaking discussions about energy needs, technological advancement, and the very nature of civilization itself.

However, such ambitious proposals are often met with skepticism, especially when they disrupt established paradigms. Critics questioned the feasibility of constructing such a megastructure given the current technological constraints and the vast resources required to surround a star. Moreover, there were concerns about what implications a Dyson Sphere held for humanity. Would it foster a sense of connection to the cosmos, or would it detach us further from our home planet—the very cradle of our species? Environmental concerns also became part of the discourse, leading to explorations about the ethical dimensions of manipulating stellar energies.

As the years passed and the scientific community began to digest Freud's audacious visions, acceptance slowly began to take root amid ongoing criticisms. Electronic designs proposing various incarnations of Dyson Sphere variations emerged, including the ideas of Dyson swarms and Dyson bubbles, each reflecting different degrees of engineering feasibility and adaptability. The discourse transitioned from that of critique to elaboration, researchers envisioning what the constituent technologies might look like. Concepts like solar energy collection through orbital panels and other engineered constructs demonstrated an adaptability to Dyson's visionary dream and helped pave the way for the exploration of renewable energy in contemporary discussions.

The reception of Dyson's theories did not occur in isolation; it influenced and was influenced by the cultural movements of its time. The 1960s and 70s, while initially stifled by Cold War tensions, also witnessed a burgeoning space race, a public appetite for exploration, and significant advancements in scientific understanding. Motivated in part by these cultural threads, thinkers and scientists began proposing practical approaches to Dyson's ideas that would extend beyond their theoretical origins. Far from being relegated to the domain of science fiction, Dyson Spheres and similar constructs began to appear as serious hypotheses that could guide future exploration.

One noteworthy evolution in reception came through initiatives like the Search for Extraterrestrial Intelligence (SETI). Drawing on Dyson's original premise that technologically advanced civilizations might have left detectable imprints through their energy-harvesting endeavors, researchers began looking beyond Earth for signs of such massive structures. This added velocity to scientific conversations about the existence of advanced civilizations and the technologies they might wield, awakening public interest and international collaboration in the field of astrophysics.

This re-framing of the Dyson Sphere within the SETI context helped shape educational curricula, stimulating student interest in astrophysics and engineering fields. Interest broadened into interdisciplinary studies, merging philosophy, ethics, and futurism with hard science, reflecting a growing understanding of how humanity's ambitions in astrophysics relate to contemporary societal challenges.

Dyson's theories catalyzed not just a shift in how we might think about space energy, but how we reconcile our technological aspirations with ethical concerns about advancement and environmental stewardship.

Moreover, Dyson's influence extended beyond academia into popular media. The notion of Dyson Spheres seeped into science fiction literature and film, embedding itself into the public consciousness as allegorical narratives that explored humanity's place in the cosmos. As writers like Arthur C. Clarke and Isaac Asimov integrated similar ideas into their narratives, they painted vivid possibilities of future civilizations where harnessing the energies of stars became a reality, evoking both hopes and existential questions about technological progress. The dialogues fostered by these narratives transcended mere entertainment, becoming cultural commentaries on the human experience and the choices we must make as we look toward our future.

The long-term impact of Dyson's ideas on contemporary science is palpable. The interest generated has led to numerous academic papers exploring various facets of the Dyson Sphere concept, from theoretical engineering to ethical considerations. Researchers have taken cues from Dyson's initial proposals in their studies, attempting to draw parallels between his theoretical constructs and advancements in renewable energy technologies, such as solar panels and other forms of harnessing stellar energy. The pursuit of sustainable energy solutions has gained urgency in face of climate challenges—paralleling Dyson's vision of effectively utilizing the vast power of the cosmos as we seek to balance our technological growth with environmental responsibility.

In the decades since, Dyson's theories have served as a catalyst for discussions on the future of humanity. They invite inquiries into the transition from a planetary civilization to a cosmic one, urging us to ponder humanity's trajectory as we stand on the precipice of larger-scale advances in energy and space exploration. The evolution of thought that his proposal inspired reverberates through contemporary inquiries into astrobiology, engineering, and socio-political aspects of global efforts to engage with the cosmos.

As the scientific community has continued its exploration of Dyson's original ideas, they have demonstrated a dynamic interplay of skepticism, acceptance, and eventual integration into broader discourse around technology and energy. This metamorphosis—cycling from skepticism to curiosity, and ultimately to serious avenues of inquiry —highlights how bold visions can catalyze transformative dialogues in science and philosophy alike. Dyson's legacy is not merely an idea; it is an unfolding narrative that challenges humanity to persistently reimagine itself, its technologies, and its engagement with the universe.

2.5. A Legacy in the Stars

Contemplating the vast realms of space exploration inevitably leads us to Freeman Dyson's profound legacy—one that transcends his lifetime and continues to shape scientific thought and technological aspirations. Dyson's concept of a Dyson Sphere has become synonymous with humanity's ambitious desire to reach beyond Earth, pushing the boundaries of our understanding of life, civilization, and the cosmos itself. His ideas not only ignited the passions of scientists and engineers but also captured the imaginations of storytellers and cultural critics, intertwining scientific inquiry with narrative exploration.

Dyson's exploration into the possibilities of megastructures, particularly the Dyson Sphere, reoriented discussions about energy consumption and planetary survival. As humanity grapples with the pressing challenges of climate change, dwindling resources, and technological integrations within our ecosystems, Dyson's proposals present an innovative vision for a future characterized by energy abundance. The very essence of his work challenges us to consider how advanced civilizations might evolve and how we must rethink our relationship with energy and its conservation.

Moreover, his ideas propelled the field of astrobiology and exoplanetary research, raising questions about the potential signs of advanced extraterrestrial civilizations. The search for Dyson Spheres or their equivalents encapsulates the broader quest to decipher the universe's secrets. In doing so, Dyson became a catalyst for interdisciplinary collaboration—bridging physics, engineering, philosophy, and beyond —as researchers across fields began to consider the implications of civilizations that might harness stellar energy. The framework he established led to meaningful inquiries into what it means to be a civilization in the cosmos—how we might define progress, significance, and our potential interactions with those beyond our planet.

One cannot overlook how Dyson's ideas have influenced contemporary space exploration initiatives. The development of solar panel technology, space habitats, and renewable energy research reflect his profound foresight. The nascent interest in mega-engineering within the scientific community exemplifies an evolution rooted in his vision —a determination to explore the construction of colossal structures that can sustain humanity beyond Earth. Today, we witness a resurgence in ambitions towards building the infrastructure needed for sustainable space exploration, be it through lunar bases or Martian colonies—all echoing Dyson's underlying philosophy of reaching for the stars.

Culturally, Dyson's legacy has seeped into the broader consciousness, influencing narratives and philosophies that contemplate humanity's role in the universe. Science fiction, once thought of merely as escapism, has become a vital medium through which to explore the socio-political ramifications of technological advancement. Authors like Liu Cixin, who discuss in detail concepts akin to Dyson Spheres and advanced civilizations in works such as "The Three-Body Problem," engage in a nuanced examination of ambition, ethics, and the cosmic scale of existence. Such narratives reflect our intrinsic desire not only to dream of possibilities but also to address the ethical concerns tied to our aspirations for expansion.

In contemplating Dyson's legacy, it becomes crucial to acknowledge the ethical dimensions embedded in his theories. As we pursue engineering marvels that span the stars, we must consider questions not just about what we can achieve, but also about what we should endeavor. The potential impacts on the environment, the dynamics of social equality, and the preservation of cultural identities are essential facets of any major scientific undertaking. Dyson's own philosophical inquiries prompt reflections on the symbiosis between technological prowess and ethical accountability.

As we continue this journey through the cosmos, the legacy of Freeman Dyson serves as both an inspiration and a guidepost. His calls for ambitious thought, curiosity, and responsibility resonate in our explorations. They challenge us to imagine not solely a future of technological marvels but one characterized by a nuanced understanding of our place in the universe, urging us to craft a narrative as expansive and intricate as the night sky itself.

Ultimately, Dyson's vision encapsulates a timeless human aspiration —the yearning to ensure that as we reach for the stars, we do so with reverence for the intricate tapestry of life and existence. His legacy propels us toward a profound understanding that our cosmic aspirations and technological endeavors must harmonize with our moral compass, guiding the trajectory of life as we navigate the spaces between stars. In this ongoing quest, we might yet discover not only new worlds filled with energy and potential but also insights that illuminate our fundamental humanity.

3. Shaping a Star: The Fundamentals of a Dyson Sphere

3.1. Harnessing Stellar Energy

Harnessing energy from stars presents one of the most tantalizing prospects fitted within the context of advanced civilizations and their technological capabilities. Central to the concept of a Dyson Sphere, this possibility invites an exploration of the immense power that such a structure could facilitate for a civilization. As we delve into the science behind capturing this cosmic energy, we discover not only the theoretical foundations but also real-world applications that could emerge from such monumental energy sources.

At a fundamental level, capturing stellar energy would rely upon the principles of thermodynamics and the nature of electromagnetic radiation emitted by stars. Every star, including our Sun, radiates energy across various spectra—infrared, ultraviolet, visible light, and more. This energy spans a vast range—our Sun alone emits approximately 386 billion billion watts of power, providing an almost limitless supply of energy when considered from a cosmic perspective. Dyson proposed that a civilization advanced enough to contemplate building a Dyson Sphere would also be able to capture and utilize a significant fraction of this energy, fundamentally reshaping its technological, economic, and social landscape.

The practicality of constructing a Dyson Sphere involves several theoretical models, all aimed at maximizing energy capture with efficiency in mind. The most fundamental design involves a spherical shell or swarm, built around a star, comprising vast arrays of energy-collecting panels or devices. A Dyson Sphere could be envisioned not as a solid shell—an implausible construction given the stresses involved—but rather as a collection of satellites or solar panels, distributed in orbit around a star, collectively absorbing its radiant energy. This concept, recognized as a Dyson Swarm, presents a more feasible approach while retaining the core idea of capturing stellar output.

The technology required for such mega-engineering endeavors would, by necessity, attain remarkable advancements in several fields. The materials selected for energy collection would need to be highly efficient, capable of withstanding extreme temperatures, radiation, and other harsh conditions present in space. Furthermore, advancements in robotics and automation would play critical roles in the construction and maintenance of these extensive structures, allowing for a self-sustaining system to grow organically as a civilization advances.

The applications of the energy harnessed from a Dyson Sphere stretch into numerous domains. Energy harvested could power entire cities, sustain extensive interstellar travel endeavors, or even facilitate terraforming efforts on other celestial bodies. Imagine a scenario where advances in propulsion technology allow spacecraft powered by immense energy sources to travel across the solar system in a fraction of the time it would take today, thereby opening new realms for exploration, colonization, and resource extraction. This would not only fulfill the energy needs of a civilization thriving within its home system but might also lead to the development of galactic industries and trade, fundamentally altering the economic fabric of that society.

Equally intriguing are the environmental implications surrounding the concept of harnessing stellar energy. If humanity achieves the capability to construct a Dyson Sphere, it would possess the potential to supply energy without relying on fossil fuels or depleting planetary resources—a crucial consideration in the context of current environmental challenges. Such a breakthrough could provide a cleaner and more sustainable energy source, inspiring future efforts to reconcile technological progress with ecological stewardship.

In addition to the physical and technological aspects, harnessing stellar energy touches on broader philosophical considerations. The act of surrounding a star with a megastructure capable of capturing its energy triggers inquiries regarding the ethical dimensions of such manipulations. While a civilization might boast unparalleled power through energy abundance, it would concurrently bear the responsibilities associated with such capabilities. What societal values would govern the use of such energy? How would they mitigate environmental impacts on their home planet if they choose to expand beyond?

Through the lens of human history, the quest for energy has often paralleled societal evolution, marking significant leaps in technology and culture. By harnessing stellar energy, we could witness a transformative leap into a new era of civilization—one where energy constraints dissolve, igniting innovation across multiple disciplines and encouraging exploratory ambitions beyond the solar system.

Colloquially, examining the intricacies tied to harnessing stellar energy allows us to appreciate the burgeoning possibilities that await. Should civilizations reach the threshold of a Dyson Sphere, the synergy of advanced technologies, ethical considerations, and energy abundance may fundamentally redefine life as we understand it—not just for the beings constructing such structures but for the broader universe teeming with potential. In this cosmic journey, the capture of stellar power may serve as the precursor to a new chapter in civilization, a chapter where humanity no longer confines itself to Earth, but instead boldly embraces its place among the stars and all the infinity that lies beyond.

3.2. Multiple Dyson Variants

The concept of a Dyson Sphere, as imagined by Freeman Dyson, is not a single entity or construction but rather an umbrella term that encompasses a variety of theoretical designs and structures devised to harness the vast energy outputs of stars. This exploration of "Multiple Dyson Variants" delves into the intricacies of these alternative constructs, examining their unique attributes, potential advantages, and the challenges they present for advanced civilizations.

At the heart of this conversation lies the distinction between different conceptual frameworks surrounding Dyson's vision, each adapted to address specific engineering, economic, and ecological challenges faced by hypothetical advanced societies. The three prominent variants under the Dyson umbrella are the Dyson Sphere, Dyson Swarm, and Dyson Bubble, each possessing distinct characteristics that could reshape our understanding of cosmic energy harnessing.

The most ambitious of these variants is the classic Dyson Sphere, envisioned as a solid shell encasing a star and maximizing energy absorption. While inherently elegant in design, the structural integrity and engineering feasibility of such an immense megastructure have raised substantial concerns within the scientific community. A fully enclosed sphere would face immense gravitational forces and thermodynamic stresses, posing significant challenges in materials science and engineering capabilities. This theoretical construct ultimately requires materials and technologies far beyond our current achievements to ensure stability and resilience against the immense heat and radiation emitted by a star.

In recognizing the drastic limitations of a solid sphere, researchers and theorists have gravitated towards the concept of the Dyson Swarm. Instead of a singular, rigid structure, a Dyson Swarm consists of numerous individual satellites or photovoltaic panels orbiting a star, creating a collective network of energy-harvesting devices. These distinct units can be designed to operate independently while collectively contributing to a larger energy-capturing system. The brilliance of the Dyson Swarm lies not only in its ability to mitigate some of the gravitational and thermal stresses associated with a solid sphere but also in providing adaptability and resilience; the deployment of additional units can scale the energy capacity according to the civilization's needs, reflecting a more sustainable approach to energy consumption.

The design of a Dyson Swarm represents a significant evolution from the sphere concept, introducing considerations about the orbital dynamics required to maintain the balance of these devices around their host star. Each satellite's orbit must be meticulously calculated to minimize collision risks while maximizing energy collection efficiency, raising new questions about governance and coordination for any civilization undertaking such a monumental effort. The challenge lies in the technological sophistication required for automated coordination and maintenance, as well as how these constructs adapt over time to maintain optimal functionality.

Another intriguing variant of Dyson's energy-harvesting possibilities is the Dyson Bubble. This concept envisions a series of lightweight, independent structures suspended around a star by solar sails—essentially a network of interconnected panels that float within a designated space. The physics of the Dyson Bubble invites considerations of the propulsion systems necessary to maintain stability and orbit around a star, opening up further possibilities of exploration and modular expansion.

As appealing as these variants are, they do not come without their own sets of challenges. Efforts to create a Dyson Bubble or Swarm still require advancements in space travel, materials, and automation far beyond current capabilities. Each variant reflects a conscious effort to balance the engineering constraints with the aspirational goals of civilization, highlighting ongoing debates among scientists about not only the feasibility but also the ethical considerations tied to such colossal undertakings.

Throughout this examination of Dyson variants, it's essential to address another critical aspect—resource allocation. The construction and maintenance of these megastructures demand extensive resources, from raw materials to energy utilization and intellectual capital. Questions about the economic models that advanced civilizations would adopt become increasingly relevant, particularly regarding sustainability and equitable energy distribution.

Moreover, a deeper analysis into the implications of varying designs reveals a potential shift in societal structures. For instance, the emergence of a Dyson Swarm could catalyze a rethinking of venture systems within a civilization, pushing for collaboration on unprecedented scales. This cooperative atmosphere could yield societal benefits fueled by shared knowledge and collective ambition. On the contrary, the construction of a single solid Dyson Sphere might necessitate a more centralized approach, challenging notions of governance and resource management.

Additionally, the environmental impact of these ventures raises complex discussions, especially concerning the delicate balance between celestial manipulation and ecosystem integrity. As civilizations strive for interstellar energies, they must tread carefully, contemplating the repercussions their structural ambitions might have not only on their own systems but also on the greater cosmic tapestry.

Ultimately, exploring Multiple Dyson Variants progresses beyond mere technical assessment; it opens a dialogue that intertwines ethics, economics, and culture. Each design choice leads to possible futures, shaping human civilization's holistic approach to energy consumption and adaptation. As we deepen our understanding of these theoretical constructs, we find ourselves challenged to envision a future where not only our energy needs are met but where harmony between technology and thoughtfulness reigns supreme, as we reach beyond the confines of our planet to engage meaningfully with the cosmos.

3.3. Engineering Beyond Limits

As we strive to construct a Dyson Sphere, the undertaking transcends mere ambition, encapsulating a series of engineering challenges and technological hurdles that would need to be overcome to realize one of humanity's grandest visions. The scale of engineering involved in creating such a megastructure poses unprecedented difficulties—each aspect of the design and construction process will require meticulous planning, innovative materials, and groundbreaking technologies. To delve into these intricacies, we must explore the multifaceted challenges associated with such a monumental endeavor.

The foundations of constructing a Dyson Sphere begin with the understanding of stellar mechanics and the dynamics of construction in a space environment. Surrounding a star necessitates not just an understanding of proximity to a sun but also the intricate balance of forces that will act on the structure itself. Gravitational forces, radiation pressure, and thermal dynamics pose critical challenges to the stability and integrity of any megastructure built around a star. The engineering must account for these forces, ensuring that the structure can withstand significant temperatures and pressures while maintaining its shape and function over unfathomable timescales.

One of the primary hurdles in this grand engineering experiment lies in material science. The materials selected must not only endure the extreme conditions surrounding a star—where temperatures can soar into the thousands of degrees Celsius—but must also afford sufficient durability against corrosion and physical degradation over eons. Today's materials often yield under high radiation exposure, requiring innovative solutions in material composition and engineering. Advances in nanotechnology and artificial materials—such as carbon nanotubes or graphene—could offer pathways to craft materials with the required resilience and thermal resistance, enabling construction techniques that are currently outside our realm of capability.

The immense scale of the Dyson Sphere presents logistical challenges that are difficult to fathom. Whether we pursue the idea of a rigid shell or a distributed swarm of solar collectors, the deployment of thousands of components into orbit requires sophisticated strategies for assembly and maintenance. Current space logistics would struggle with the volume of materials required for such a project, suggesting the necessity of new methods for transportation within our solar system. Innovative propulsion systems and potentially even modular manufacturing facilities in orbit or on planetary bodies might need to be engineered, allowing for the gradual assembly of components far from Earth.

Constructing a Dyson Sphere also involves multifaceted technological advancements in robotics and automation. The sheer complexity of the task means that human labor alone would be insufficient; instead, fleets of autonomous robots capable of adapting to the harsh conditions of space and performing intricate assembly operations would be essential. These robotic systems would need to be designed for robustness, with the ability to self-repair or replicate as needed, facilitating the long-term maintenance of the structure. Additionally, artificial intelligence could play a pivotal role in optimizing the operations and managing the logistics of constructing and maintaining a Dyson Sphere.

Energy management emerges as another prominent consideration in the quest to construct a Dyson Sphere. Harnessing stellar energy efficiently entails designing systems capable of converting vast amounts of light into usable power without excessive loss. The efficiency of energy conversion and distribution across multiple systems would require innovations in photonic technologies, energy storage solutions, and transmission lines capable of sustaining distances that dwarf those we experience on Earth. This technological leap must also embrace sustainable practices, considering how the energy collected can power other components of the Dyson Sphere and possibly even back on Earth, creating a seamless energy network.

Societal implications also intertwine with engineering efforts. The coordination of a civilization's efforts toward a Dyson Sphere presents societal challenges in governance, labor structuring, and resource allocation. As we scale our technological capabilities beyond terrestrial capacities, collaborative frameworks—and possibly even new economic models—would be necessary to manage the breadth of the endeavor. Concepts of ownership, stewardship, and communal responsibility regarding the Dyson Sphere would need to be established, fostering a culture that embraces such ambitious ventures sustainably and ethically.

Finally, there is the critical aspect of testing and validating theoretical designs before any practical construction can begin. Prototyping elements of the Dyson Sphere, perhaps through smaller test projects such as solar arrays in orbit or advanced materials studies, could illuminate pathways for efficient construction. Theoretical models must also be substantiated through simulations that account for variable astrophysical phenomena, scalability, and potential contingencies that might arise over the lifespan of such structures.

In conclusion, the engineering of a Dyson Sphere poses myriad challenges that stretch our current technological capabilities. However, this immense undertaking encapsulates the spirit of exploration and innovation that defines humanity's quest to transcend its limitations. Each obstacle surmounted in this frame creates new opportunities for advancements not only in our pursuit of cosmic energy but also in our understanding of engineering, sustainability, and what it means to inhabit the stars. As we navigate these ambitious engineering considerations, we redefine not just the boundaries of our capabilities but envisage a future where human ingenuity resonates amidst the cosmos, illuminating the path toward our stellar aspirations.

3.4. Material Science in Space

Material science is at the forefront of humanity's journey into space, particularly when it comes to the monumental task of constructing and maintaining advanced structures such as a Dyson Sphere. The complex environmental conditions found in the cosmos pose significant challenges for material technologies, requiring innovative solutions to withstand extreme temperatures, radiation, and the vacuum of space.

In the context of a Dyson Sphere, the materials chosen must fulfill several critical requirements. First and foremost, durability is essential. Materials must resist degradation caused by exposure to solar radiation and cosmic particles, which can ionize atoms and alter material properties over time. Current materials, like metals and plastics, may not possess the requisite longevity, necessitating the development of advanced composites or alloys. For instance, research into carbon-based materials, including graphene and carbon nanotubes, presents promising avenues due to their exceptional strength-to-weight ratios and resilience to heat and radiation.

Next, the thermal properties of materials become paramount. A Dyson Sphere would exist in a thermal environment significantly different from that found on Earth, often subjecting structures to extreme heat during exposure to sunlight. Reflective and insulating coatings capable of managing thermal loads will be necessary to protect not only the structure but also any equipment or habitats situated within the Dyson Sphere. Advanced engineering will need to focus on developing materials that can efficiently manage heat distribution, perhaps by utilizing phase-change materials that absorb or release thermal energy in response to changing conditions.

The fabrication methods for these materials will also differ dramatically from traditional manufacturing processes employed on Earth. In a microgravity environment, the behaviors of molten materials differ from those under normal gravitational conditions, leading to unique challenges and potential benefits. For example, manufacturing techniques like additive manufacturing, or 3D printing, can be adapted to utilize in-situ resources, allowing for the creation of components directly from materials found in asteroids or other celestial bodies. This method would reduce the need to transport vast quantities of materials from Earth, aligning with sustainable practices in space exploration and engineering.

Moreover, the interdependence of diverse material properties must be understood and harnessed. Engineers must not only consider strength and thermal conductivity but also weigh factors like weight, flexibility, and resistance to corrosion. Developing multifunctional materials that can perform multiple functions—such as serving as structural supports while also providing thermal insulation and radiation shielding—could lead to substantial innovations in the construction of a Dyson Sphere or similar megastructures.

The societal implications of such advancements in materials science extend into the realm of ethics and resource allocation. As we venture into space and consider the construction of monumental structures, we must deliberate on how these advancements will be utilized. The potential for resource extraction from other celestial bodies—whether asteroids, moons, or planets—challenges our understanding of ownership and stewardship. How materials will be sourced, and who has the rights to these cosmic resources is a question that must be carefully navigated to ensure equitable access and responsible management.

In terms of the broader impact on exploration and potential colonization, advancements in material science can significantly augment our capabilities to build habitats or energy-harvesting structures in hostile environments. For instance, materials that can withstand Martian dust storms, with strong resistance to abrasion and degradation, will be indispensable for human exploration and settlement on planets beyond Earth. As such, the potential to develop and deploy sophisticated materials quickly translates into expanded horizons for humanity's interstellar ambitions.

As we embark on this journey toward constructing a Dyson Sphere, our understanding and application of material science will pave the way for monumental engineering feats. The innovations spurred by this pursuit will undoubtedly have ripple effects across various fields, reshaping not only our approaches to space exploration but also redefining our terrestrial manufacturing processes and sustainability efforts. Through this lens, material science remains a cornerstone of our aspirations to harness the energy of the stars and ensure the survival of humankind in the vast landscape of the universe.

3.5. Power Dynamics

The prospect of harnessing the immense power generated by a Dyson Sphere opens a complex web of power dynamics that could redefine relationships within a civilization and its interactions with the cosmos. As humanity contemplates the feasibility of constructing such a megastructure, it becomes imperative to consider how the vast quantities of energy collected will be utilized, distributed, and governed. This exploration of power dynamics will illuminate the societal, political, and ethical implications of living with a Dyson Sphere.

Firstly, the power dynamics surrounding a Dyson Sphere are largely predicated on the sheer magnitude of energy it could generate. Capturing a star's energy output, which for our Sun is approximately 386 billion billion watts, means that any civilization capable of building a Dyson Sphere would likely experience an unprecedented abundance of energy. This raises fundamental questions regarding the management and governance of such wealth. Would power dynamics shift towards centralization, where a dominant authority controls energy distribution, or would new decentralized frameworks emerge, allowing for a more equitable sharing of resources?

In contemplating the organizational structure that would manage energy harvested from a Dyson Sphere, various models could manifest. A centralized approach may resemble modern corporate or governmental structures, where energy is allocated based on consumption and social stratification. This could lead to economic disparities, where those with privileged access to energy resources dominate, potentially leading to societal unrest or rebellion among the disenfranchised.

Conversely, a decentralized model could foster democratic governance of energy production and usage, allowing communities or smaller factions to control localized energy production. The "commons" approach might envision a system where the abundance generated by the Dyson Sphere becomes a shared resource, negotiated and regulated collectively. Such a structure could foster collaboration, innovation, and sustainability, as energy becomes less a commodity and more a lifeblood for all, reducing conflict over resources.

However, governance structures are not the only dynamic in play. The introduction of abundant energy from a Dyson Sphere could catalyze advancements in technology, including breakthroughs in automation and artificial intelligence. As machines take on more responsibility for energy management and distribution, socio-political dynamics would shift further, creating questions of oversight and accountability. Would these advanced systems operate independently of human influence, or would there remain a necessity for human governance over these technologies?

Additionally, the nature of energy production could also impact societal hierarchies. In many cultures throughout history, power has often derived from resource control. Should civilization wield the energy from a Dyson Sphere, traditional hierarchies might be challenged or transformed. Job markets could shift dramatically, as energy-centric industries evolve alongside innovations in technology and automation. New professions may emerge in engineering, maintenance, and energy management, while obsolete roles could fall by the wayside, creating potential economic tensions and necessitating significant societal adaptation.

Furthermore, the implications of energy abundance extend beyond economic dimensions into ethical realms. The ability to harness star power raises moral questions regarding stewardship of resources. A civilization that manages this energy must grapple with its responsibility towards environmental sustainability and conservation. How energy is used—whether for exploration, industry, or to support life itself—will undoubtedly reflect the values and ethics of that society. A technocentric civilization focused on expansion could lead to exploitation of both extraterrestrial resources and ecosystems, while a more mindful civilization might prioritize balanced co-existence with nature, emphasizing ecological considerations.

Another critical aspect of power dynamics involves the impact on interstellar relationships. Should a Dyson Sphere become a reality, the energy output it generates could facilitate travel to other star systems, expanding humanity's reach into the cosmos. The energy wealth from a Dyson Sphere could empower significant exploratory efforts, but it also necessitates a careful approach to contact with potentially advanced extraterrestrial civilizations. Humanity would need to navigate the complexities of engagement, weighing the benefits of collaboration against the risks of dominance or cultural imperialism.

The broader implications of power dynamics within the cosmic context also influence perspectives on extraterrestrial life. The existence of Dyson Spheres could alter how we philosophically engage with the search for intelligent life in the universe. As advanced civilizations capable of harnessing stellar energy become a focal point of inquiry, our understanding of what constitutes intelligence or advancement may evolve significantly. Here, the energy dynamics of one civilization may create ripples of concern and curiosity across light-years, as we ponder whether energy abundance correlates with moral wisdom, ecological responsibility, and sustainability.

Moreover, these power dynamics underscore vital communal considerations around the governance of celestial megastructures. As multiple civilizations explore engagement within the cosmic tapestry of existence, questions regarding ownership, jurisdiction, and ethical stewardship of energy resources must be addressed. The construction of a Dyson Sphere could lead to disputes over the control of energy—a highly sought-after commodity on a galactic scale. How humanity balances its ambitions for cosmic energy with ethical obligations to other forms of life will be a defining aspect of this power dynamic.

In summary, the power dynamics surrounding a Dyson Sphere embody an intricate interplay of governance, ethics, and societal evolution. The monumental energy produced not only holds the potential for transformative advancements in technology and society but also carries with it profound responsibilities and complexities that must be navigated thoughtfully. As we imagine a future shaped by such extraordinary constructs, we must confront these dynamics with a blend of ambition, caution, and ethical reflection, ensuring that our cosmic aspirations harmonize with a commitment to sustainable progress and communal well-being. Exploring these dimensions invites us to ponder not just how we might capture the energy of a star but how we can evolve as stewards of our capabilities—both on Earth and among the stars we strive to explore.

4. Historical Inspirations and Realities

4.1. From Star Trek to Scientific Theories

The imaginative cosmos of science fiction has long served as a fertile ground for scientific inquiry and theoretical exploration. Indeed, the fascination with the idea of Dyson Spheres—a concept proposed by Freeman Dyson as a means for advanced civilizations to capture the energy output of stars—has roots deeply embedded in speculative narratives that ignite human curiosity and ambition. From early science fiction tales to contemporary cinematic portrayals, the depiction of megastructures like Dyson Spheres has not only captured public imagination but has also inspired real-world scientific endeavors.

In the advent of contemporary scientific discourse, the idea of a Dyson Sphere resonates far beyond its theoretical beginnings in Dyson's paper in 1960, "Search for Artificial Stellar Sources of Infrared Radiation." The mind of Freeman Dyson himself was undoubtedly influenced by earlier science fiction works that toyed with the bounds of technology and the cosmos. The genre of science fiction, while often dismissed as mere entertainment, has a vibrant history of forecasting technological possibilities that later find themselves mirrored in genuine scientific exploration.

Prominently featured in works of science fiction are sprawling constructs reminiscent of Dyson's vision. Arthur C. Clarke's narrative in "Rendezvous with Rama" presents advanced extraterrestrial civilizations and their awe-inspiring engineering feats, hinting at ideas that echo Dyson's proposal. Similarly, Larry Niven's "Ringworld" explores a megastructure encircling a star, alluding to the practical implications of living amidst the vastness of space. Each tale broadens the scope of discussion around civilizations that strive to build and harness such constructs for energy, growth, and exploration.

The direct correlation between these narratives and the scientific exploration of megastructures is evident in how speculative ideas often pave the way for formal theories and studies. The ambitions laid out in early works of science fiction frequently serve as precursors to the hypotheses of scientists and engineers. For instance, the speculative technologies proposed for Dyson Spheres have echoed through various research initiatives, incentivizing advancements in fields such as astrobiology, materials science, and astrophysics. The conceptual framework for Dyson Spheres often employs a blend of scientific conjecture and creative liberty—merging the lines between fiction and scientific exploration, enticing researchers to imagine the possibilities.

Furthermore, the integration of Dyson Sphere concepts into the cultural fabric has had a reciprocal effect on scientific pursuits. As Dyson's ideas gained traction, they found their way into popular media, making their way into documentaries, educational programs, and even mainstream films that portray humanity's quest for energy sustainability in an age of increasing ecological consciousness. This popularity amplifies human curiosity and intent toward exploring such ambitious constructs, bridging the chasm between theoretical physics and societal aspirations.

The role of the Search for Extraterrestrial Intelligence (SETI) also cannot be overlooked in this context. The idea that advanced civilizations might create megastructures to harness stellar energy has led researchers in the field to consider Dyson Spheres as potential indicators of extraterrestrial technology. SETI actively investigates celestial phenomena for signs of such structures as they scout for signals from intelligent life. The notion of Dyson Spheres, once simply a figment of speculative fiction, has now emerged as a legitimate scientific inquiry spurred on by the narratives that preceded it. The advancements in technologies, such as deep-space scanning and spectroscopy, are reflections of this legacy—tools once dreamt of in fiction that now forge paths into the cosmos.

Moreover, as we strive for new frontiers in engineering and materials science, we find that the imaginative constructs of fiction demand rigorous consideration of feasibility. Contemporary researchers harness creativity as a catalyst for scientific innovation—interpreting the challenges posed by Dyson-like structures in fresh and exciting ways. Groundbreaking research into orbital solar panels, advanced energy storage systems, and autonomous robotic technologies often borrows inspiration from narratives originating in science fiction, demonstrating a delicate synergy between the realms of imagination and empirical reality.

In this spirit, it becomes evident that the engagement with the idea of Dyson Spheres and related megastructures fuels a continuous dialogue between speculative fiction and scientific rigor. As humanity ponders its place in the cosmos and the potential for interstellar civilizations, the implicit messages found within our stories kindle exploration and curiosity. This dialogue points towards a future marked by innovation where the creative visions of artists, writers, and scientists collide to forge pathways into the unknown.

By legitimizing countless possibilities through their narratives, science fiction serves to effectively shape our scientific endeavors while igniting passions for exploration. "From Star Trek to Scientific Theories" underscores how deeply intertwined our technological pursuits are with the imaginative landscapes of old, marking a promising terrain where human creativity and scientific inquiry converge in the quest for a brighter relationship with the cosmos. With each step we take driven by inspiration, we remind ourselves that dreams are precursors to reality—that the fabric of our aspirations can indeed translate into the engineering feats of the future.

4.2. Societal Impact and Perspectives

The cultural and societal impact of the concept of Dyson Spheres and other hypothetical megastructures extends far beyond the realms of hard science and engineering, permeating various aspects of human thought, creativity, and social structures. This exploration addresses how these grand ideas resonate within the collective consciousness, fuelling imaginations and inspiring new narratives across literature, art, philosophy, and popular media. Dyson Spheres, initially a bold theoretical proposition for energy collection advanced by Freeman Dyson, serve as potent symbols of humanity's aspirations towards mastery over cosmic forces and encapsulate the profound interplay between our technological ambitions and ethical responsibilities.

In literature, the proliferation of futuristic megastructures, like Dyson Spheres, provides fertile ground for writers to speculate about the implications of advanced civilizations that operate on a scale unimaginable to contemporary societies. These constructs often represent the intersection of human ingenuity and the very essence of existence in a universe filled with possibilities. From the grand narratives woven by masters of science fiction like Arthur C. Clarke and Isaac Asimov to contemporary authors engaging with the potentials of cosmic dwelling, the imagery of vast structures encircling stars evokes a profound sense of wonder, inspiring readers to imagine scenarios where humanity transcends its earthly confines.

Moreover, the societal implications encapsulated in these narratives reflect ongoing concerns about environmental sustainability, technological equity, and the moral dimensions of expansion and exploration. As authors grapple with the consequences of harnessing stellar energy, they create complex characters and societies whose struggles mirror real-world anxieties about resource distribution, governmental control, and ecological impacts. These literary explorations encourage readers to contemplate not only the possibilities of living among the cosmos but also the ethical frameworks that must guide such aspirations.

Art also plays a vital role in reflecting and shaping the societal impact of Dyson Sphere concepts. Visual artists, driven by the challenge of representing the unfathomable scales of cosmic structures, often use metaphors to connect viewers to the underlying themes of exploration and existential inquiry. Artistic interpretations of Dyson Spheres can evoke a sense of awe and reverence, prompting reflections on humanity's place amid the vast universe. Moreover, their artworks often weave together scientific thought with emotional resonance, encapsulating the dual nature of our aspirations: the relentless pursuit of progress alongside the cautious understanding of our responsibilities.

The cultural ramifications extend into popular media, where films and television often utilize Dyson Sphere-like constructs to examine broader themes about identity, power, and the human experience. Visually striking depictions of these megastructures offer audiences a glimpse into potential futures, sparking discourse about the practicalities and ethical dilemmas of advanced engineering. Through dystopian or utopian narratives, creators explore the societal impacts of stellar energy harnessing, compelling viewers to confront their own values and visions for the future.

Beyond the realm of artistic expression, the ideas surrounding Dyson Spheres catalyze conversations about the societal structures and cultural paradigms that may arise in the pursuit of grand cosmic endeavors. The concept of energy abundance opens discussions about the possible socio-economic systems that could emerge among civilizations capable of harnessing such resources. The juxtaposition between centralized power structures and decentralized models for equitable energy distribution becomes rather poignant, urging societies to contemplate their values and governance systems. Would energy from Dyson Spheres fuel cooperation and cultural exchange, or would it lead to further stratification and inequality?

Moreover, Dyson's vision of harnessing stellar energy invites philosophical inquiry into ownership, stewardship, and what it means to be a responsible civilization. The questions raised about the ethics of colonizing resources—whether they be from distant stars or other celestial bodies—compel societies to reflect on their relationship with the universe. Engaging in debates around the stewardship of megastructures encourages humanity to consider the potential legacy of their actions and the moral imperatives tied to their pursuits.

As the scientific community continues to explore the theoretical underpinnings and practical applications of Dyson Spheres, societal discourse escalates alongside. Discussions about advancements in technology, environmental responsibility, and interstellar ambitions frame a collective desire to make informed choices about the future. Such dialogues emphasize the importance of fostering interdisciplinary collaboration, merging the insights of scientists, ethicists, artists, and storytellers as we navigate the complexities of cosmic exploration.

In conclusion, the societal impact of the Dyson Sphere concept transcends its theoretical foundations. It weaves together a rich tapestry of creative expression, ethical inquiries, and cultural reflections that shape how humanity envisions its place within the cosmos. As we continue to dream of energy-harnessing megastructures, we must be vigilant in considering the values and responsibilities that accompany such aspirations, ensuring that our journey into the stars is defined not only by technological advances but also by a commitment to ethical stewardship and the well-being of the universe we seek to explore.

4.3. Realizing a Hypothesis

In the quest to understand the universe and our place within it, hypothesizing about cosmic megastructures like the Dyson Sphere serves both a theoretical and practical purpose. Realizing a hypothesis —specifically, the existence of structures capable of harnessing stellar energy—requires a blend of scientific inquiry, technological innovations, and collaborative efforts across disciplines. As we embark on this multifaceted journey, we are prompted to consider various avenues of research, testing, and validation aimed at establishing the credibility of such grand designs.

The first essential step in this exploration involves the collection of observational data. Efforts undertaken in modern astronomy are crucial for identifying possible signs of Dyson-like structures beyond our solar system. One of the most pressing methods includes the study of infrared radiation emitted by distant stars. Dyson's original proposition highlighted that advanced civilizations capable of constructing megastructures would emit waste heat detectable as infrared signatures. Therefore, astronomers utilize infrared detectors to survey stars, searching for unusual energy patterns that might indicate the presence of dense energy-collecting structures.

Institutions such as the Kepler Space Telescope and the upcoming James Webb Space Telescope represent monumental strides in this area. Their enhanced capabilities allow scientists to explore the cosmos with unprecedented precision, documenting exoplanetary systems and analyzing their spectral signatures. Through these analysis techniques, researchers can determine whether the energy profiles of certain stars exhibit anomalies consistent with the hypothesis of Dyson Spheres. Identifying excess infrared light, for instance, may lead to conjecturing that an alien civilization is harnessing stellar energy, prompting further investigation.

The methodologies of SETI (Search for Extraterrestrial Intelligence) harness a complementary approach by actively listening for signals or communication patterns that would imply the existence of advanced civilizations. SETI's research not only aims to discover engineered signals within the cosmos but also leans toward recognizing the broader environmental indicators, such as Dyson Sphere-like constructs. Should researchers pinpoint distinct patterns or irregularities in energy emissions from certain stars, they would investigate whether such phenomena correlate with advanced engineering.

Moreover, key mathematical models help frame the search for Dyson Spheres by allowing scientists to simulate how energy-harvesting constructs might affect their stellar environments. Theoretical frameworks grounded in astrophysics and thermodynamics guide researchers in evaluating energy flows, radiation profiles, and even the gravitational impacts of hypothetical megastructures. These models aid in refining the parameters and expectations for observational missions, enhancing our capacity to detect alien technologies embedded in the universe.

Another avenue of potential realization lies in the advancements of probe technology. Sending autonomous probes equipped with sophisticated sensors to distant star systems offers another layer of understanding. These deep-space missions could provide tangible evidence of energy absorption systems, providing a direct means for validation. In tandem with astronomical observations, deploying probes may yield the crucial insights needed to either substantiate or challenge the existence of Dyson-like constructs unequivocally.

Furthermore, as curiosity about Dyson Spheres grows, interdisciplinary collaboration among physicists, engineers, ecologists, and ethicists becomes increasingly essential. Each perspective contributes vital insights into understanding the broader implications of such structures—not just in terms of construction but encompassing their societal, ethical, and ecological ramifications. As humanity grapples with energy concerns here on Earth, discussions fueled by the hypothesis of Dyson Spheres encourage innovative approaches to sustainable practices and tech advancements.

Ultimately, the endeavor of realizing a hypothesis about Dyson Spheres embodies the persistence of human curiosity. It intertwines empirical science with philosophical inquiry, challenging us to expand our imagination and broaden our pursuits into the cosmos. Through astronomical observations, theoretical modeling, technological advancements, and collaborative endeavors, society moves closer to a greater understanding of what it might mean to inhabit a universe rich with potential. The realization of hypotheses, particularly concerning life beyond our sphere, serves as a testament to human aspirations aimed at unraveling the mysteries enveloping us—a quest for knowledge that continues to propel us into the vast uncertainties of space. More than a scientific inquiry, it embodies the very essence of what it means to be part of a larger cosmic tapestry, urging us to seek connections not just among the stars but within the shared journey of all existence.

4.4. SETI and Dyson Spheres

The Search for Extraterrestrial Intelligence (SETI) is at the forefront of humanity's quest to locate potential signs of intelligent life beyond our world, and it has long been intertwined with the exploration of Dyson Spheres. The idea of Dyson Spheres, proposed by Freeman Dyson in 1960, reflects a profound understanding of how advanced civilizations might harness the energy output of their host stars. This notion has sparked the imagination of scientists and futurists alike, driving an exploration not merely of our technological capabilities but of our place in the cosmos and the potential existence of other life forms.

SETI operates under the premise that while we seek recognizable signals from alien civilizations, we might also observe the physical manifestations of their technological prowess—such as Dyson Spheres. These constructs, designed to maximize energy capture from stars, could emit infrared radiation as a byproduct of their operation. Thus, researchers have turned to the skies, employing infrared telescopes and observational data to identify anomalies around stars that could suggest sophisticated energy-harvesting structures.

The foundational principle of SETI rests upon the concept that advanced civilizations, particularly those on a path of technological growth, may evolve to a point where they consume energy on a massive scale. Dyson's hypothesis illuminates a possible future wherein a civilization fully envelops its star to capture energy, generating a distinct signature that could be detectable from Earth. This highlights an intrinsic connection between the concept of Dyson Spheres and the goals of SETI: both endeavors aim to discern the patterns that characterize intelligent life and gauge its potential existence across the universe.

To ground this premise in empirical research, the approach involves scanning other solar systems for evidence of Dyson-like structures. By focusing on stars exhibiting unusual infrared emissions or patterns inconsistent with natural stellar behavior, scientists can narrow down their search for potential artificial constructs. For instance, the discovery of the peculiar stellar dimming behavior of KIC 8462852, often referred to as "Tabby's Star," stirred interest as researchers investigated whether it could be an artifact of a massive structure, possibly indicative of an advanced civilization. Although subsequent investigations proposed more natural explanations for the observed anomalies, they nonetheless underscore the fascinating linkage between cosmic phenomena and potential extraterrestrial technologies.

Moreover, advances in astronomical technology have equipped researchers with powerful tools allowing for comprehensive investigations of distant stars. Projects utilizing space-based observatories capable of high-resolution imaging and detailed spectrum analysis serve as critical assets in the pursuit of understanding if civilizations might exist capable of constructing Dyson Spheres. The deployment of new missions such as the James Webb Space Telescope will bolster our observational capacity, bringing us a step closer to answering whether we share the universe with other intelligent beings.

Yet the search for Dyson Spheres and the broader quest for extraterrestrial intelligence extend beyond mere observations; they pose fundamental questions about our understanding of life and civilization. Upon contemplating the existence of advanced civilizations capable of engineering such structures, we are reminded of the profound implications those findings would have on human philosophy, ethics, and societal progress. If evidence of extraterrestrial civilizations arises, it invites renewed scrutiny of our responsibilities as stewards of our planet and potential ambassadors to the cosmos.

Furthermore, the pursuit of understanding Dyson Spheres has prompted discussions about the nature of progress and technological ambition among civilizations. If we were to discover that such megastructures exist, it would ignite curiosity about the cultures and values that fostered their creation. Would these civilizations operate on principles of sustainability and balanced coexistence, or would they exemplify a cautionary tale of technological exploitation? The complexities surrounding these ethical inquiries compel us to reflect on our paths of development, our energy consumption practices, and our interactions with our environment.

As humanity moves forward, a comprehensive investigation into Dyson Spheres through SETI's lens will undoubtedly shape our strategies for understanding the universe. The merging of technological exploration with philosophical contemplation encourages a holistic approach as we strive to unlock the mysteries of cosmic existence. Each signal detected, each anomaly observed, fuels a persistent inquiry into whether we are alone or merely at the precipice of joining a broader tapestry of civilizations, each one chasing their aspirations amid the stars.

The pursuit of extraterrestrial life and the exploration of Dyson Spheres serve as not only scientific inquiries but as reflections of humanity's enduring desire to connect with the cosmos, urging us to explore outside our planetary confines and strive for knowledge beyond our current horizon. Embracing this journey challenges us to envision a future where we are not just passive observers of the universe, but active participants in its unfolding narrative, enriched by every possibility that lies within the vast, interstellar unknown.

4.5. Beyond the Speculative

The exploration of Dyson Spheres and similar megastructures is not merely a theoretical exercise in astrophysics; it embodies humanity's relentless pursuit to understand our place in the cosmos and the potential for a future beyond Earth. As we delve deeper into this subject, we encounter profound questions regarding the very nature of civilization, the essence of progress, and the ethical implications of our technological aspirations. The real challenge lies not only in the engineering and scientific complexities but also in how we navigate the speculative ideas that emerge from these cosmological phenomena.

At the heart of this discourse is the fine balance between speculation and empirical research. Scientists must navigate a landscape fraught with uncertainties, where the boundaries of known science intersect with theoretical possibilities. This interplay drives the scientific community to ask questions that extend beyond immediate observational capacities, leveraging conjecture as a tool for exploration. For instance, discussions around Dyson Spheres naturally stimulate inquiries into potential advanced civilizations capable of creating such constructs, prompting researchers to rethink not only what constitutes intelligence but also the values that would govern such societies.

As we progress into this speculative realm, it's crucial to recognize the significance of interdisciplinary approaches. The blending of astrophysics with philosophy, ethics, sociology, and even art fosters a holistic understanding of what the implications of constructs like Dyson Spheres might entail. How they might reshape our understanding of energy consumption, environmental stewardship, or societal structures becomes an engaging area where science meets the humanities. This collaboration allows for a richer exploration of consequences that arise from human ambition projected onto a cosmic scale.

In this context, scientists are tasked with not just validating theories through empirical means but also engaging with the broader societal impact of their work. The promise of harnessing energy on the scale of a star raises questions about the equitable distribution of resources and the responsibilities tied to such power. What implications would arise from our capability to tap into near-boundless energy? How would this reshape economic systems, political governance, and even cultural narratives surrounding growth and development? These considerations are as critical as the scientific undertakings to build the technologies that would regulate and enable such megastructures.

Furthermore, the quest for understanding Dyson Spheres invites a philosophical inquiry into the nature of reality itself. Our engagement with the cosmos reflects a desire to transcend the limitations of our existence, urging us to ponder deeper existential questions. How do we define life? What does it mean to flourish in a universe filled with potential life forms—some perhaps using energy in ways we have yet to imagine? These reflections are vital as they inform the ethical frameworks that must accompany our cosmic exploration.

Moreover, as we stand on the precipice of potential realizations of these grand hypotheses, we are increasingly aware of our role as both observers and participants in this cosmic narrative. The reality is that our technological advancements must be paired with a commitment to sustainable practices and an awareness of our responsibilities as stewards of the universe. The construction of megastructures like

Dyson Spheres will not only reflect our engineering capabilities but also challenge us to harmonize ambition with ecological mindfulness.

Thus, beyond the speculation lies the call for a deeper understanding and collaboration across disciplines—one that pervades scientific inquiry, philosophical reflection, and cultural expression. In pursuing these lofty ideas, we must ensure that our visions for the future of humanity are grounded in ethical contemplation, ecological awareness, and a commitment to fostering life in all its forms across the cosmos. The intersection of human ambition, cosmic curiosity, and ethical consideration illuminates a path forward—a journey that transcends the boundaries of Earth and leads us to embrace the stars not merely as distant objects of fascination but as integral partners in our quest for understanding and existence.

5. Cosmic Implications: A Paradigm Shift

5.1. Redefining Civilization

In contemplating the far-reaching implications of a Dyson Sphere, we find ourselves tasked with redefining what civilization means in the context of advanced energy harnessing. Historically, civilization is often marked by its ability to manipulate and utilize energy sources effectively. Therefore, the introduction of a Dyson Sphere—an immense structure capable of capturing the energy output of an entire star—invites a reevaluation of our foundational concepts of societal development, sustainability, and the very history of technological progress.

At the heart of this redefinition lies the sheer scale of energy abundance afforded by a Dyson Sphere. Our current energy infrastructures, characterized by the extraction of fossil fuels and reliance on renewables like solar and wind, present significant limitations in terms of capacity and sustainability. In contrast, a Dyson Sphere could provide nearly inexhaustible energy, fundamentally altering the economic and social structures of a civilization. Imagine a world where energy scarcity is a relic of the past—where power is virtually limitless, allowing for unprecedented technological innovations and societal advancements. Civilization as we know it would no longer be bound by the same constraints and struggles that currently mandate the management of energy resources, leading to a society that might focus more on exploration, creativity, and collaboration rather than survival.

As we envision a future shaped by such abundant energy, potential societal transformations emerge. The shift toward a civilization unencumbered by energy scarcity could catalyze a transition from hierarchical power dynamics based on resource control to more egalitarian frameworks that promote equitable energy distribution. Governance models centered around energy utilization might evolve, allowing for a reconfiguration of political structures that prioritize sustainability and collaborative decision-making over competition and exploitation.

Such a transformation has the power to redefine authority within societies, leading to a more democratic, participatory approach to governance that encourages innovation and progress.

In contemplating the ethics surrounding the construction and utilization of a Dyson Sphere, we are confronted with complex dilemmas. Who owns the energy harvested from a star? In a civilization that has achieved such technological prowess, the concept of ownership may evolve beyond mere possession toward a shared stewardship model. This shift necessitates a cultural embrace of responsibility —where individuals and communities are not just beneficiaries of energy abundance but active participants in sustainable practices. Such community-centered philosophies can potentially foster cooperation, cultural evolution, and holistic progress within societies capable of reaching the stars.

Furthermore, the implications for how we interact with neighboring celestial bodies and potential extraterrestrial life will be profound. The existence of a Dyson Sphere serves as a double-edged sword: it holds the promise of energy independence for humanity while raising ethical questions about the exploitation of other worlds and civilizations. The recognition of interstellar ecosystems as interconnected leads to a paradigm shift, prompting civilization to consider its responsibilities toward such entities. As we expand our reach in the cosmos, our understanding of what it means to coexist and collaborate expands alongside it.

Redefining civilization in the realm of the Dyson Sphere thus leads us to engage more broadly with the philosophical implications of our existence. The very act of creating a construct capable of harnessing stellar energy introduces inquiries into our identity, purpose, and legacy as a species. Questions surrounding life's value, the ethics of advancement, and the condition of technological growth become central to this discourse, necessitating reflections on the values we choose to embody as we expand our influence amongst the stars.

The pursuit of realizing a Dyson Sphere aligns not just with scientific ambition but with a deeper quest for meaning, purpose, and understanding in the universe. It prompts us to rigorously evaluate not only our technological aspirations but also the principles, ideals, and responsibilities that will shape our interactions in this new cosmic paradigm. As humanity contemplates its place among the stars, we embark on a journey of redefining civilization—one that harmonizes our unwavering ambition with our profound ethical obligations, ensuring that our energy-filled future reflects the very best of our collective humanity. In sum, the Dyson Sphere is not merely an engineering feat but a potential linchpin in reshaping civilization's story—a story that embraces the interconnectedness of all life and the cosmos that nurtures it.

5.2. Energy Abundance

Energy abundance represents a pivotal paradigm shift for human civilization, particularly as we advance technologically toward the possibility of constructing a Dyson Sphere—or equivalent megastructures capable of harnessing the energy output of stars. This transition from limited energy resources to a virtually limitless supply raises profound implications for societal development, environmental sustainability, and human advancement.

At the core of this shift is the reimagining of how societies function in response to abundant energy. Currently, energy scarcity drives nations, communities, and individuals to compete over finite resources. This competition often exacerbates inequalities and engenders conflicts, as energy availability directly correlates with economic stability and societal well-being. With the advent of a Dyson Sphere, the fundamental dynamics of energy economics could transform dramatically. A civilization capable of harnessing the vast energy output of a star could reframe its relationship with not only energy but also with equity and prosperity. In a reality where energy is abundant, societies might redirect their focus from merely survival and competition toward innovation, creativity, and exploration.

Moreover, the implications of energy abundance extend to environmental considerations. Traditional energy production methods often lead to significant ecological degradation and climate change, as societies extract fossil fuels and generate waste while managing critical ecosystems. The proliferation of clean, renewable energy sources, such as those harnessed from a Dyson Sphere, could enable societies to transition towards more sustainable practices. This shift might reduce humanity's carbon footprint, mitigate global warming, and foster a renewed respect for planetary health. The potential for widespread adoption of renewable energy technologies would diminish reliance on fossil fuels, empower ecological regeneration efforts, and result in a symbiotic relationship between civilization and nature.

This abundant energy supply could also facilitate unprecedented exploration of the cosmos. As advanced technologies arise from energy abundance, humanity could embark on ambitious interstellar exploration missions, extending its reach beyond the solar system and unlocking the potential for resource acquisition from other celestial bodies. This expansion could unlock new frontiers in scientific discovery and technological innovation, fostering a deeper understanding of the universe and our place within it. In this new paradigm, the aspirations of humanity might transcend terrestrial limitations, allowing societies to dream bigger and explore the depths of the cosmos.

However, while energy abundance presents exciting possibilities, it also raises critical questions regarding governance, social structures, and ethical considerations. As societies adapt to this newfound bounty, the challenge will be to ensure equitable distribution of resources and the maintenance of social cohesion. The tension between centralization and decentralization of energy management systems will remain prevalent; attention must be given to how power dynamics and authority structures might shift. It becomes essential to prioritize democratic participation and accountability in decisions relating to the use of abundant energy, thereby avoiding pitfalls where disparities and disenfranchisement resurface in new forms.

Ethical questions surrounding the stewardship of energy also emerge. An abundant energy supply may tempt societies to overreach in their consumption or exploitation of resources. Ethical frameworks will need to guide decision-making, ensuring that advancements are approached with a sense of responsibility toward future generations and ecological balance. The challenge lies in reconciling ambition with mindful stewardship, where human exploration is balanced by a commitment to preserve the integrity of the cosmos and other celestial bodies.

Furthermore, the cultural adaptations required to embrace a future defined by energy abundance could reshape societal values. A collective consciousness that prioritizes sustainability, cooperation, and ecological mindfulness will need to emerge, as humanity navigates the complexities of interstellar expansion. Arts, literature, and philosophical discourse must reflect these shifts, encouraging a narrative that emphasizes holistic approaches to progress. A cultural renaissance could bloom, grounded in narratives that encourage unity with the universe rather than exploitation, shaping a new ethos for generations to come.

In conclusion, energy abundance presents an extraordinary potential for drastically altering the trajectory of human civilization. As we contemplate the implications of harnessing stellar energy through constructs like the Dyson Sphere, we recognize that the journey is not merely about capturing energy but also about redefining our relationship with it and the cosmos. We stand at a crossroads where the choices we make today will reverberate throughout the future, challenging us to envision a sustainable, equitable, and enriched society as we embrace the boundless possibilities that energy abundance may provide.

5.3. Technological Leap Beyond Ourselves

Achieving the construction and functionality of a Dyson Sphere represents not just a technological milestone but a monumental leap beyond our current capabilities. In order to transform this hypothesis into reality, we would need several advancements across various fields of science and engineering, as well as a cultural shift in how we perceive our relationship with energy and the cosmos. These technologies must be resilient, scalable, and adaptable, ensuring both long-term sustainability and efficient energy management on an astronomical scale.

At the core of this endeavor lies advanced energy collection and conversion technology. Current solar panels, while effective on Earth, fall short when it comes to the vast scale and efficiency required to harness the energy of a star such as our Sun. To realize a Dyson Sphere, we would require energy-collection devices that are resilient to extreme temperatures and radiation, as well as capable of maximizing energy absorption. Innovations like space-based solar photovoltaic cells, coupled with efficient energy conversion systems, could lead to the development of arrays that can capture and convert solar energy into usable power effectively.

Moreover, the solutions must encompass a diverse range of energy management systems. Energy storage will be critical, as there will need to be mechanisms capable of holding immense quantities of energy, ready to be deployed as needed. Current battery technologies need a revolutionary overhaul to move beyond their limitations. Researchers would need to develop advanced superconductors or new materials capable of long-term energy storage without significant losses. This energy could then be transmitted efficiently through transmission lines designed to handle the immense loads derived from a Dyson Sphere, integrating seamlessly with existing energy grids or providing power to far-flung operations and colonies.

The engineering challenges extend to transportation and construction on a grand scale. The logistical demands of constructing a Dyson Sphere are staggering. It would necessitate the development of spacecraft with advanced propulsion technologies, such as nuclear thermal propulsion or even theoretical concepts like antimatter drive systems, to transport materials from Earth and possibly even asteroids or other celestial bodies. The ability to mine and utilize extraterrestrial materials will be essential; therefore, asteroid mining technologies would need to be refined and implemented to ensure a steady supply of resources.

Automated systems will play a significant role in the construction and maintenance of a Dyson Sphere. Advanced robotics will be indispensable, particularly in constructing functions that operate in the harsh environment of space, where human labor is less feasible. Autonomous construction robots could assemble components in orbit around a star, utilizing advanced AI algorithms to adapt to the dynamic challenges presented by the environment. This leap would involve innovations in swarming robotics and self-repairing materials, allowing for a continuously evolving structure that can adapt over time.

Research into material science would also need to take significant strides to provide the necessary enhancements for durability, resistance to space radiation, and thermal stability. New materials, such as metamaterials or nanostructures, could play a pivotal role in the design and resilience of the solar-collecting components of a Dyson Sphere. Their utility would come not only from their physical properties but also from their functionality in a variety of environmental conditions, potentially combining several characteristics into one adaptable solution.

Culturally, realizing a Dyson Sphere will necessitate a societal leap in how we view our place in the universe and our responsibilities toward it. The collective mindset must pivot towards sustainability and stewardship over energy resources, guiding the ethos that drives the construction and utilization of such colossal projects. It will require education and engagement across all sectors, encouraging collaborative efforts and multi-disciplinary dialogue.

Moreover, we must consider the ethical implications of wielding such power. The societal framework around energy equity, resource management, and the relationship between civilization and the cosmos would need to evolve leapingly. This transformation will involve dialogue at all levels—from policymakers to individual citizens—bestowing a higher degree of ethical responsibility on our relationship with energy and our environments.

In summary, the journey towards constructing a Dyson Sphere is rife with challenges that span scientific, engineering, and ethical domains. By strategically aligning advancements in technology with a profound cultural shift, we can start to envision a future where our civilization not only reaches for the stars but also embraces the profound responsibilities that such aspirations entail. This leap is not merely about achieving technical feats; it is about crafting a new understanding of life within the grand tapestry of the universe, one that harmonizes our actions with the celestial forces that nourish us.

5.4. Economic and Political Challenges

The advancement of technology and societal structures necessary to conceptualize and potentially build a Dyson Sphere or similar megastructures opens the door to an expansive array of economic and political challenges. Building such a formidable structure requires not only unprecedented technological and engineering feats but also substantial economic frameworks to support those endeavors, along-side political systems that can effectively manage the sociocultural transformations that will ensue.

At the heart of these challenges is the economic model that would govern the construction and maintenance of a Dyson Sphere. Given the colossal investments of time, resources, and human capital required, the question arises: who will finance such a venture? Traditional funding sources, such as private corporations and national governments, may struggle to mobilize the necessary capital for an undertaking that exceeds current paradigms of investment. As a result, we might observe the emergence of new economic models focused on collaborative funding mechanisms, potentially through international partnerships or public-interest conglomerates aiming to pool resources for common benefit.

One possible solution could be the advent of a new "space economy" based on celestial resources. As humanity moves toward interplanetary and interstellar exploration, asteroids and other celestial bodies could serve as novel sources of raw materials. Extracting materials from these bodies may not only sustain the construction of a Dyson Sphere but could also provide the economic impetus to initiate projects of such immense scale. The establishment of space mining initiatives could lead to new markets and economic relationships, effectively breaking free from Earth-centric resource dependencies. This shift could render energy scarcity obsolete, positively impacting global economies and prompting political re-evaluations of resource management and distribution.

However, the realization of such projects raises complex political implications. The geopolitical landscape may shift dramatically as nations might vie for supremacy in space exploration, seeking to claim territories and resources beyond Earth's atmosphere. Questions about ownership rights over extraterrestrial materials will ignite fierce debates, potentially leading to conflicts reminiscent of historical territorial disputes on Earth. Therefore, international agreements and cooperative treaties—much like the Outer Space Treaty of 1967 —would need to evolve to address the intricacies of ownership and stewardship of celestial resources, establishing norms that respect both human interests and the preservation of extraterrestrial environments.

In addition to space economy dynamics, the transition to a post-scarcity society driven by the principles of Dyson Sphere economics might incite radical political changes. The abundance of energy captured from stars could render traditional power dynamics obsolete, shifting focus from scarcity-driven competition to collaborative governance aimed at equitably distributing resources. Such a transition might encourage the establishment of decentralized political models emphasizing communal governance or new global coalitions advocating for sustainability and common good. The potential for energy abundance could thus foster more inclusive political structures aiming to prioritize the welfare of citizenry and address pressing global challenges, from climate change to poverty.

Moreover, the technological advancements underpinning Dyson Sphere construction raise important questions surrounding labor and governance. The sheer scale of automation and robotics required for assembly and maintenance could displace a significant portion of the workforce traditionally engaged in energy production and resource extraction. Consequently, societies would need to navigate the socio-economic fallout of widespread automation—restructuring education, training, and labor markets to equip individuals with skills suited for a new economy built around cosmic engineering and resource management.

While envisioning a potential future characterized by energy abundance and a thriving space economy is enticing, it is essential to also recognize the ethical implications that accompany these changes. The power dynamics within a society using an energy-intensive Dyson Sphere cannot overlook the potential for inequality to resurface—where elite factions might have disproportionate access to the wealth generated through stellar energy harnessing. Preventing these disparities from crystallizing would require vigilant governance structures, civic engagement, and proactive policies prioritizing equity.

In summary, the economic and political challenges surrounding the construction of a Dyson Sphere are vast and multifaceted. They encompass the need for new funding structures, the reimagining of global resource management, and evolving power dynamics that focus on collaboration rather than competition. Additionally, societies must grapple with an ethical imperative to ensure that the benefits of such cosmic ventures are equitably shared, fostering a culture of care and responsibility worthy of the monumental aspirations tied to living and thriving among the stars. The interplay of these factors will ultimately shape humanity's path as we traverse from our planet into the cosmic expanse.

5.5. Environmental and Ethical Considerations

The construction of a Dyson Sphere, an audacious endeavor aimed at harnessing the entirety of a star's energy output, brings forth a plethora of environmental and ethical considerations that force us to reckon with our responsibilities as advanced civilizations. At its core, this megastructure represents not just an achievement in engineering and technology, but also a profound undertaking that intersects with the ecological balance of its host star system and the ethical dimensions of our ambitions.

To begin with, the environmental implications of constructing such a massive structure around a star are manifold. Enveloping a star changes the dynamics of energy distribution within that solar system and would alter the functioning of planets, moons, and other celestial bodies that rely on the star's light and heat for their ecosystems. By capturing a significant fraction of a star's energy, we risk disrupting the delicate balance that has allowed life to flourish on those celestial bodies. Questions arise regarding the ecological impacts on neighboring planets—will their climates change, and how will biospheres adapt to a diminishment in solar energy? The foundation of life as we know it could be jeopardized if the energy harvesting is not managed thoughtfully.

Furthermore, the materials used in constructing a Dyson Sphere raise another layer of environmental concerns. The extraction of raw materials from planets or asteroids must be conducted with great care to minimize ecological damage. The mining of extraterrestrial bodies to source construction materials poses risks of habitat destruction, contamination, and resource depletion. The ethical implications extend beyond our solar system as well—if we were to colonize other planets for resources, how would we ensure responsible stewardship of those environments? Engaging in mega-engineering projects invites debates on whether humanity has the right to manipulate and potentially exploit other worlds, and what responsibilities come with such capabilities.

The operational phase of managing a Dyson Sphere introduces additional ethical considerations. How would such a civilization ensure that this immense resource wealth is distributed equitably? A major concern is the potential for inequalities to emerge as those who control the Dyson Sphere's energies could exercise power over those who do not or cannot access those resources. Governance structures would need to evolve to ensure that the abundance of energy does not lead to exploitation and oppression, maintaining a balance where technological advancements serve the common good rather than concentrate power among a select few.

Moreover, with great power comes great ethical responsibility. Harnessing the equivalent energy output of a star would create profound opportunities, but it also brings the moral imperative of using that energy in ways that prioritize sustainability and benefit all sentient beings within the system. This compels societies to adopt ethical frameworks that dictate how energies are consumed, fostering practices that reflect a commitment to ecological and social responsibility.

In a broader context, the creation of a Dyson Sphere raises existential questions about humanity's role in the universe. With the capability to manipulate stellar energy comes the opportunity to reflect on our values and aspirations as a species. Should such a structure become a reality, it could signify a departure from a resource-strapped survival mindset to one where we foster interstellar cooperation and exploration. This relationship with cosmic resources may redefine habitats, civilizations, and potentially influence our relationship with any other advanced civilizations we may discover.

Ethics also extends to the implications of potential contact with extraterrestrial life. If advanced civilizations capable of constructing Dyson Spheres exist, how would we navigate relationships with them? Would our presence within the cosmic community reflect a legacy of respect and cooperation, or would it mirror past colonial interactions on Earth fraught with exploitation and hubris?

Reflecting on these environmental and ethical considerations is paramount as we push the boundaries of technology and exploration. In contemplating such grand designs as the Dyson Sphere, we must engage deeply with our responsibilities toward life, ecosystems, and universal coexistence. Our technological pursuits should not only aim to capture energy but also to cultivate wisdom, fostering a relationship with the cosmos that prioritizes sustainability and respects the life forms that may inhabit it. As we stand on the threshold of potential cosmic engineering feats, the more pressing questions emerge: how do we evolve into responsible stewards of the energy that powers the stars, and how do we ensure our journey leaves a positive mark on the universe rather than a destructive one?

6. Cultural Reflections on Megastructures

6.1. Influence on Art and Literature

Throughout history, the profound mysteries of the universe have inspired artists, writers, and intellectuals to express their thoughts and emotions creatively. The notion of Dyson Spheres, as a transformative megastructure capable of harnessing the energy of an entire star, stretches the imagination and has permeated various artistic and literary endeavors. In this exploration of cultural reflections, we delve into how the concept of Dyson Spheres influences and shapes creative expression, revealing our innermost hopes, fears, and aspirations regarding our place in the cosmos.

The narratives and themes woven into literature about stellar energy capture often explore the balance of technological aspirations and the ethical dilemmas that accompany them. Renowned science fiction authors have utilized Dyson Sphere-like constructs as a mechanism to convey both utopian visions and cautionary tales. This juxtaposition reflects humanity's dual nature: our relentless pursuit of progress and the accompanying risks and responsibilities of wielding such power. Authors who envision the implementation of Dyson Spheres often explore the fate of civilizations that pursue energy on a vast scale, probing the consequences of their actions and encouraging readers to contemplate the value of sustainability and ethical stewardship.

One prominent example in literature is Arthur C. Clarke's "Rendezvous with Rama," where the discovery of a massive cylindrical spaceship brings questions of advanced technology and its potential consequences to the forefront. As characters navigate their understanding of this immense structure, readers are prompted to reflect on the impact of such technologies on human existence and interstellar relationships. The allure of harnessing energy from a Dyson Sphere mirrors the intrigue of exploring alien megastructures—a theme echoed across various narratives that center on humanity grappling with the implications of extraordinary advances.

Similarly, the visual arts capture the awe and wonder evoked by the idea of Dyson Spheres. Artists have sought to give form to these abstract concepts, employing imagination to translate the enormity of such constructs into tangible, visceral experiences. The creation of vibrant illustrations and installations portraying Dyson Sphere-like structures invites viewers to engage with the speculative possibilities presented by such feats of engineering. These artistic interpretations evoke a deep connection to the cosmos, emphasizing humanity's desire to explore and understand our surroundings while symbolizing the quest for energy and growth.

The influence of Dyson Spheres also extends to philosophy, as the idea provokes profound existential questions about our place in the universe and the potential for alien intelligence. In various philosophical works, thinkers reflect on the implications of building a megastructure devoted to energy harnessing and what this reveals about humanity's character and ambitions. The discourse extends to the potential ethical ramifications of encountering advanced extraterrestrial civilizations that may have developed similar structures. What common ground could exist among diverse life forms that harness stellar energy? Would such encounters reveal shared values or highlight fundamental differences in how to engage with the cosmos?

The cultural reflections surrounding Dyson Spheres resonate deeply with the societal anxieties and ambitions faced by contemporary civilization. As societies grapple with pressing environmental concerns and the need for sustainable energy, the dream of a Dyson Sphere serves as a metaphor for transcending immediate limitations. Literature, art, and philosophy collectively reinforce the notion that our aspirations for cosmic energy must be anchored by ethical stewardship and conservation of both our planet and beyond. The interplay of these disciplines encourages us to reflect on how we envision humanity's future among the stars, searching for harmony between technological ambition and a commitment to coexistence.

In addition to the speculative dimensions, the storytelling surrounding Dyson Spheres often serves as a mirror reflecting humanity's hopes and fears. Discovering that we are not alone in the universe —especially as indicated by potential Dyson Sphere constructions— could challenge our understanding of ourselves and our role among the stars. These reflections compel us to cultivate a sense of responsibility for our planet and any extraterrestrial counterparts we may encounter in the future. The narratives we create encourage us to rise to the occasion and foster a universal narrative that extends beyond survival, nurturing a sense of community among all intelligent beings.

In summary, the influence of Dyson Spheres on art and literature serves as a powerful conduit through which humanity grapples with its aspirations, challenges, and responsibilities as a technologically advanced species. By weaving together imaginative constructs with fundamental ethical inquiries and philosophical reflections, we can better understand our place within the cosmos. As we envision a future defined by the wonders of stellar energy harnessing and the inherent complexities it brings, we remain committed to cultivating our understanding of what it means to be part of a larger interconnected universe, nurturing hope, creativity, and responsibility as we embark on this cosmic journey.

6.2. Religious Interpretations and Philosophies

Throughout history, humans have sought meaning in the cosmos, often finding clarity through religious interpretations and philosophies that revolve around the mysteries of existence. The concept of a Dyson Sphere—a theoretical construct capable of harnessing the vast energy output of a star—offers fertile ground for exploring profound implications within religious and philosophical frameworks. As we delve into these interpretations, we can see how ideas surrounding the construction and existence of such advanced megastructures can illuminate our understanding of divinity, purpose, and humanity's overarching place in the universe.

Religious interpretations of Dyson Spheres may initially seem abstract, but they invite us to reconsider the relationship between humanity and the cosmos. For many faith traditions, the universe is often viewed as a purposeful creation imbued with meaning—a divine reflection of higher truths. The creation of a Dyson Sphere could arguably align with divine stewardship, representing humanity's quest not only to understand creation but also to partake in the active shaping of that creation. There's a subtle yet significant connection between the act of harnessing stellar energy and the age-old religious tenets surrounding creation myths, caretaker roles, and divine intentions. In this light, the construction of a Dyson Sphere could be interpreted as humanity's extension of the Creator's hand—a tangible expression of our embedded role in the unfolding cosmic narrative.

In contrast, the ambitious nature of constructing a Dyson Sphere also brings to mind the biblical notion of hubris—the perils associated with overreaching human ambition. The Tower of Babel, for example, serves as a cautionary tale about humanity's attempt to reach the heavens and attain divinity through sheer construct. If one views the Dyson Sphere as a metaphor for striving beyond established limits, it invokes considerations about the moral and ethical implications of such endeavors. As societies attempt to shape and control cosmic forces, they may confront the question of whether this ambition reflects enlightenment or transgression. This duality reflects broader philosophical inquiries about the nature of power and the human condition: do we aspire to create in harmony with the cosmos, or do we risk becoming lost in our ambitions, neglecting the humility that the universe demands?

Philosophically, Dyson Spheres challenge traditional concepts of existence and purpose. The mere idea of a civilization harnessing the energy output of a star compels philosophies of progress and futurism. In existential terms, the construction of a Dyson Sphere provokes inquiries about humanity's role and significance in an expansive universe—addressing questions about what it means to be a conscious, creative species capable of such grand advancements. This discourse intricately connects to existentialist thought, where the pursuit of meaning in an indifferent or chaotic universe becomes a defining inquiry. The potential for living among the stars, powered by the colossal energy of Dyson Spheres, could represent not only survival but flourishing—a testament to human potential when it's harmonized with cosmic forces.

Meanwhile, the notion of cosmic unity emerges through philosophical explorations of Dyson Spheres, inviting reflections on the interconnectedness of existence. By envisioning a life interconnected through shared energy harnessed from stars, humanity might conceive of a new cosmopolitanism, one that extends beyond earthly boundaries and nurtures a sense of belonging within the universe. This philosophical evolution could lead to emergent ideas surrounding collective stewardship—where technologies like Dyson Spheres embody a commitment to shared existence, sustainable practices, and universal ethics that transcend individual cultures.

Moreover, the lens of futurism also captures religious and philosophical interpretations surrounding Dyson Spheres. Eschatological beliefs—those that reflect on end-times or ultimate destinies—may evolve with the prospects of harnessing stellar power. Concepts of resurrection or ascendance could be reimagined through the lens of technological advancements, exploring how such constructs align with evolving spiritual beliefs about transcendence and unification with the divine. Humanity's journey toward the stars invokes reflections about the continuation of life beyond Earth, the nature of immortality, and the quest for a legacy that resonates in both temporal and eternal contexts.

The ethical ramifications of envisioning Dyson Spheres intertwine with both religious and philosophical frameworks as well. As societies embark on this monumental journey to harness cosmic resources, a critical inquiry emerges: how can moral frameworks guide our pursuit of energy abundance? The pressing need for stewardship, equity, and ecological compassion resonates with many religious teachings and philosophical doctrines that emphasize the ethical treatment of all living beings. Individuals and communities may face complex moral dilemmas regarding resource allocation, environmental sustainability, and the treatment of ecosystems and potential extraterrestrial life.

Ultimately, the implications surrounding Dyson Spheres within religious interpretations and philosophical discourse offer a rich tapestry of inquiries regarding existence, purpose, ethics, and interconnectivity. As we explore the potentials of living among the stars, we confront vital questions about our relationship with the cosmos and the responsibilities that accompany such transformative ambitions. Through the lens of faith and philosophy, we can begin to envision not only the structural feats we might accomplish but also the deeper truths that govern our journey as we strive to manifest our cosmic aspirations harmoniously and ethically. The quest for Dyson Spheres may thus serve as a means to unite humanity in its enduring search for meaning within the vast and mysterious universe.

6.3. Utopian and Dystopian Views

Utopian and dystopian views regarding Dyson Spheres serve as compelling narratives reflecting humanity's hopes and fears as we grapple with the concept of these monumental constructs. Throughout creative works, discussions surrounding these megastructures often frame them within the scope of how they might profoundly alter human life, not only in terms of energy access but also in societal organization, environmental impact, and our very relationship with the cosmos.

In utopian portrayals, Dyson Spheres are seen as beacons of hope —a means to unlock vast energy reservoirs that could lead to a flourishing era for humanity. These narratives emphasize the transition from energy scarcity to abundance, inviting the possibility of a global society centered around sustainability and equity. The structures become representations of human ingenuity, showcasing our capability to transcend limitations and challenges posed by our planetary existence. With the energy harvested from a Dyson Sphere, the potential exists to eradicate poverty, eliminate energy-related conflicts, and foster environments where creativity, exploration, and collaboration flourish.

Imagine a world where the abundance generated by such a megastructure allows humanity to not only meet its energy needs but also to invest in arts, sciences, and technologies that enhance life quality. Utopian perspectives envision sprawling cities powered sustainably, societal structures based on parity and shared resources, and a civilization that recognizes itself as an integral part of a larger cosmic community. These visions suggest that, if managed equitably, the energy harvested from stars could usher in an age of enlightenment, allowing us to shift our focus from survival to thriving, ultimately reuniting humanity with the principles of harmony, balance, and stewardship of resources.

Conversely, dystopian interpretations explore the terrifying possibilities of what might happen if such immense power were concentrated in the hands of the few. The richness of energy harvested from a Dyson Sphere could lead to grave socio-economic inequalities, where a select group maintains control over resources while the majority languish in deprivation. This scenario raises critical questions regarding ownership, governance, and ethics in the age of celestial energy harnessing. As societies potentially fracture under the weight of inequality, the hope that a Dyson Sphere represents may swiftly devolve into despair as competition, greed, and exploitation take center stage.

Dystopian narratives also caution against humanity's hubris. The tale of a civilization reaching out to distant stars only to manipulate their resources selfishly serves as a reminder of past mistakes—colonization, environmental degradation, and disregard for ecological balance can all echo in these future scenarios. Writers and artists delve into the darker implications of megastructures: what if such endeavors lead to environmental collapse or the destruction of ecologies on planets that once thrived under their star's warmth? The darker portrayal serves as a powerful warning against unchecked technological ambition divorced from ethical consideration.

In truth, these contrasting narratives about Dyson Spheres encapsulate a broader conversation about the trajectory of human civilization. They force us to confront fundamental questions about technology as a force for good or a potential harbinger of chaos. The sheer scale of a Dyson Sphere serves as a canvas upon which we paint our perceptions of progress, power, and responsibility.

The impact of these perspectives stretches into the artistic and philosophical realms as well. Literature, film, and visual arts abound with representations and explorations of Dyson Spheres as tools of potential societal transformation, embodying the complexities and paradoxes of our existence. They allow us to examine our relationship with power, the responsibility that comes with technological capacity, and the importance of ethical stewardship towards our planet and beyond.

In contemplating the implications of building and living with a Dyson Sphere, we find ourselves reaffirmed as architects not only of technology but of our fate. These megastructures ultimately become reflective of our collective aspirations and our fears, inviting us to envision and construct a future informed by the lessons of the past —a future where humanity may truly harness the wonders of the cosmos responsibly, allowing diversity and flourishing to operate within a context of sustainability. In a time when environmental crises loom and energy demands escalate, the narratives surrounding Dyson Spheres remind us of our profound duty to seek solutions that harmonize with both our ethical imperatives and the environment of our home.

6.4. Concepts of Ownership and Stewardship

Ownership and stewardship are concepts deeply intertwined with the idea of Dyson Spheres and other hypothetical megastructures that span across astronomical scales. As we contemplate the implications of constructing and living with such monumental structures, we are confronted with substantial socio-political ramifications that shape our understanding of resources, governance, and our responsibilities toward both celestial and terrestrial environments.

The fundamental question of ownership begins with the origins of the resources required to construct a Dyson Sphere. Where do the materials necessary for such a grand endeavor come from, and who has the right to claim them? The notion of ownership in space complicates existing terrestrial legal frameworks and challenges our traditional views on resource extraction. While treaties like the Outer Space Treaty govern the exploration and use of outer space, questions remain regarding the extraction of minerals from asteroids or moons and whether celestial bodies can be owned by any nation or entity. Stepping into the cosmos to extract resources necessitates a robust discussion about stewardship—an ethical commitment to care for these celestial entities while utilizing their potential.

Expanding on this discourse, we must consider the way resources might be allocated and regulated in the context of ownership. If a civilization aspires to build a Dyson Sphere, the urgent need for raw materials will likely compel it to engage in discussions of governance that prioritize equitable access and sustainability. The model of ownership must evolve from one that is hierarchical and monopolistic to one that embodies communal or collective stewardship. This evolution requires establishing systems of governance that ensure resources are used justly, allowing diverse communities to benefit from their natural inheritance without degradation or exploitation.

As the energy harnessed from a Dyson Sphere becomes abundant, the implications on societal structures and power dynamics are profound. The concentration of energy resources in the hands of a few could lead to significant disparities. Therefore, collaborative frameworks must emerge, fostering cooperative governance that empowers individuals and communities to regulate resource usage collectively while holding accountable those who manage them. This necessitates a cultural shift in perception—transforming the view of ownership from individual entitlement to a shared responsibility.

Moreover, the ethical questions regarding ownership and stewardship become increasingly urgent when we consider the interactions with any potential extraterrestrial life forms that could inhabit the regions surrounding a Dyson Sphere or other megastructures. How do we approach the existence of other sentient beings within our own cosmic exploratory endeavors? Understanding ourselves as active stewards rather than mere owners of the universe will likely shape how we engage with such unidentified intelligences. The notion of universal citizenship—a recognition that we share the cosmos with other life forms—prompts ethical dialogues about non-interference, respect, and reciprocity.

Environmental stewardship also plays a critical role in the context of ownership associated with megastructures. As we take significant steps towards harnessing energy from a star, pressing questions arise regarding the ecological consequences of doing so. Could the act of enveloping a star disrupt celestial systems and ecosystems that depend on its energy? The ethical implications compel us to consider how our capabilities to shape energy resources must be accompanied by a commitment to preserving the integrity of those systems. Stepping into the role of responsible stewards requires us to adopt practices that minimize harm, promote sustainability, and respect ecological balances, echoing our responsibilities to both the cosmic and earthly environments.

This exploration of ownership and stewardship positions us at a pivotal juncture in addressing the future of our civilization in the cosmos. It intertwines our technological ambitions with ethical considerations, compelling a reconsideration of what it means to be a responsible actor on the universal stage. As we venture beyond our planetary confines, embracing concepts of communal ownership and active stewardship will be essential for navigating the complexities of existence amid the vast, uncharted territories of the universe. Such discussions not only illuminate the challenges associated with megastructures but ultimately demand a reflection of our values, shaping a narrative that intertwines advanced technological capability with a profound sense of moral responsibility.

6.5. A Mirror to Humanity's Potential

The vision of a Dyson Sphere transcends mere scientific curiosity; it acts as a mirror to humanity's potential, reflecting our deepest hopes, fears, and aspirations. In contemplating such a monumental construct, we grapple with an array of questions that speak to the essence of what it means to be human, to reach for the stars, and to understand our place in the vastness of the universe.

To embark on this journey is to confront the expansive potential of our technological aspirations. A Dyson Sphere symbolizes not just an engineering marvel but a testament to what humanity could achieve through collaboration, innovation, and vision. It compels us to reflect on our inherent capabilities and the responsibility that accompanies them. The ambition to harness the energy of a star is emblematic of a species yearning not only for survival but for transcendence—an urge to push beyond the limitations that bind us to our home planet. In this light, the Dyson Sphere stands as a beacon of hope, inspiring future generations to continue dreaming, exploring, and innovating.

Yet, amid our aspirations, there lurks an undercurrent of apprehension. The notion of encompassing a star with a structure raises profound ethical questions. What does it mean to manipulate celestial forces? Are we prepared to thread the delicate line between progress and exploitation? As we envision our future entwined with such immense power, we must confront our own nature—our tendencies toward greed, conflict, and short-sightedness. The very prospect of a Dyson Sphere becomes a reflection of our potential downfall if we fail to temper our ambitions with wisdom and care.

The implications of pursuing a Dyson Sphere stretch far beyond technical feasibility; they touch the very fabric of our social, political, and ethical landscapes. Who will control the energy that is harvested? How might such power reshape societal hierarchies? Will we establish systems that promote equity and stewardship, or will we risk repeating the mistakes of our history? These questions propel us into a reflective space where technology and ethics become inextricably linked, emphasizing the importance of governance structures that prioritize collective well-being over individual gain.

Moreover, as we delve into the dream of living among the stars, we find ourselves grappling with existential questions about our existence and purpose. The sheer scale of a Dyson Sphere compels us to think about our humanity in relation to the cosmos—a prompt to consider whether we are solitary voyagers in an indifferent universe or part of a larger cosmic community. These reflections urge us to explore the possible existence of extraterrestrial intelligences and the shared destiny that might bind newcomers to their celestial neighbors.

Envisioning the construction of a Dyson Sphere transforms our understanding of civilization and its potential trajectories. It challenges us to imagine societies that prioritize sustainability, collaboration, and harmony with the cosmos over dominance and exploitation. This potential paradigm shift affirms our capacity for growth and understanding, prompting us to consider new models of energy distribution, resource ownership, and environmental stewardship—frames that honor the interconnectedness of life across the universe.

At the heart of the discussion around Dyson Spheres lies the human narrative—our story of growth, struggle, and the pursuit of meaning. As we navigate the complex interplay between aspiration and ethics, progress and caution, we stand at a crossroads that could redefine our future. The Dyson Sphere beckons us to step beyond our terrestrial confines not merely as engineers of energy but as custodians of the cosmos—fostering a vision that recognizes our shared responsibility for all life as we reach toward the stars.

In conclusion, the concept of a Dyson Sphere encapsulates the essence of humanity's potential. It prompts us to dream boldly while remaining rooted in ethical reflection, to aspire for greatness while honoring the interconnected fabric of existence. As we look forward to a future filled with possibilities, we must remember that our advancement must be tempered with humility and stewardship, forging a narrative that envisions a sustainable and harmonious relationship with the universe—a legacy that celebrates the very best of our human experience.

7. A Philosophical Odyssey: Humanity's Position in the Cosmos

7.1. Existential Reflections

Throughout history, humanity has confronted existential questions, often propelled by our relentless quest for understanding and meaning. With the theoretical notion of a Dyson Sphere—a colossal construct designed to harness the energy of an entire star—we find ourselves facing profound reflections on our existence, purpose, and relationship to the universe. This megastructure invites us to ponder not only its potential implications on energy and technological advancement but also how such ambitions resonate within the deeper currents of human experience.

As we contemplate the possibility of a Dyson Sphere, we are prompted to reassess the boundaries of our anthropocentric worldview. Historically, civilization has defined itself through the lens of scarcity and competition, relentlessly battling for resources and status. However, the very existence of a Dyson Sphere offers a tantalizing vision—transforming scarcity into abundance and redefining our concept of success. This shift urges us to reconsider what constitutes meaningful progress. Are we merely creators of technology, or are we meant to become custodians of our universe? As we fantasize about energy harvesting on an astronomical scale, we are nudged to recognize our potential for cooperation and stewardship over exploitation and domination.

The act of constructing a Dyson Sphere, an endeavor requiring extraordinary collective intelligence and collaboration, symbolizes a new chapter in human history—one where cooperative efforts bridge the divides that have long separated us. In fostering interdisciplinary dialogue among scientists, philosophers, artists, and citizens, we come together to collaboratively shape our existential goals. This convergence of ideas could lead to a renewed sense of purpose that extends beyond the individual, promoting collective well-being and the aspiration for a thriving interstellar civilization.

However, it is critical to acknowledge the ethical dilemmas under-lying such ambitions. As we pursue the construction of a Dyson Sphere, we are confronted with the implications of wielding immense power over celestial energy. The potential for unequal distribution of resources and hierarchies echo our historical patterns of behavior, raising questions about how best to navigate this newfound abun-dance while upholding principles of equity, respect, and responsibil-ity. Our shared journey into the cosmos reflects both our aspirations and vulnerabilities, and how we choose to confront these ethical challenges will undeniably shape the fabric of our future.

Moreover, the prospect of living within a Dyson Sphere or using its energy sources compels us to confront our cosmic solitude. If humanity reaches the point of building such a structure, what does that imply about our understanding of life and intelligence in the universe? Would we remain isolated, or might we discover life forms that have traversed similar paths toward energy harnessing? Engaging with these questions encourages a profound humility and recognition of our place within a vast cosmic tapestry—reminding us that the pursuit of knowledge and power is inherently tied to bonds of responsibility and respect for the life that exists beyond our world.

Eventually, the intriguing proposition of a Dyson Sphere leads us into a deeper philosophical inquiry: what does it mean to be human in light of cosmic possibilities? Our journey toward the stars challenges ingrained narratives about limitation and isolation, inviting us to reframe our understanding of existence. This exploration offers path-ways to concepts of posthumanism—a future where our definitions of humanity evolve as we integrate technology into our essence, allowing us not only to transcend our biological constraints but also to redefine our relationships to other life forms, both terrestrial and extraterrestrial.

In contemplating the existence of a Dyson Sphere, we traverse an odyssey of existential reflections that reveal the depth of human aspiration. This not only reinvigorates our commitment to progress but also compels us to root our advancements in an ethical foundation that promotes cosmic stewardship, celebrating our shared humanity against the backdrop of a boundless universe. As we engage in these discussions and imaginings, we underline the true power of the human spirit—the ability to dream, create, and contemplate our purpose amid the stars, weaving together individual narratives into a collective journey of discovery and connection.

7.2. Cosmic Solitude or Community?

The question of cosmic solitude or community invokes a deep examination of humanity's position in the cosmos and the profound implications of theoretical megastructures like the Dyson Sphere. As we envision a future where such colossal constructs could harness the energy output of stars, we are compelled to reflect on what these advancements signify for our existence: are we solitary explorers in a vast, indifferent universe or part of a rich, interconnected community of life?

The very existence of a Dyson Sphere, in its hypothetical form, suggests not just the potential for energy abundance but also hints at the possibility of advanced civilizations with whom we may share the cosmos. If we can construct such a structure, we must interrogate the implications of other civilizations potentially doing the same. This inquiry propels us into the exploration of existence beyond mere survival—challenging us to consider the existence of other intelligent beings who might inhabit the universe and engage in similar quests for energy, knowledge, and existence.

Interestingly, the notion of community in the cosmos can manifest through shared aspirations and collective advancements in technology. Should we discover Dyson Spheres—or their equivalents—created by extraterrestrial intelligences, it would fundamentally reshape our understanding of life beyond Earth. Such encounters may foster a sense of kinship as we realize that civilizations, regardless of their origins, might converge upon the same solutions to cosmic challenges. The contemplation of constructing a Dyson Sphere compels us to visualize a harmonious interconnectedness among multiple intelligences navigating the fabric of the universe, embodying a shared pursuit of progress and sustainability.

However, the realization of this interconnectedness leads us to ponder the darker implications of such advancements. The potential for cosmic competition and conflict must not be underestimated. If Dyson Spheres are markers of advanced civilizations, then we must confront the existential threats posed by these advanced entities. Cosmic communities may harbor malevolent intentions or oppressive tendencies, casting shadows over the ideal of a harmonious shared existence. The balance between communal aspirations and the authentic reality of intelligent life in the cosmos beckons us to develop preemptive ethical frameworks that can govern our interactions.

Furthermore, the concept of cosmic solitude emphasizes the loneliness that may accompany the pursuit of ambitious technological projects. As we venture further into space, fueled by the prospect of Dyson Spheres, we must also confront the potential isolation of our species. The vastness of the universe can evoke a sense of insignificance, suggesting that despite our capabilities, we may remain alone in our pursuits. Will we find solace in the knowledge that we are capable of such feats, or will we grapple with existential angst in the face of a seemingly indifferent cosmos?

The balancing act between community and solitude prompts us to reflect on our terrestrial connections. The awareness of our shared humanity fosters a sense of responsibility to preserve the unity of our own societies as we explore the potentials of cosmic ventures. The pursuit of Dyson Spheres or other grand engineering projects should not distract us from addressing the injustices and disparities experienced within our planet's communities. Indeed, our expansions into the cosmos underscore a need for internal harmony—one that ensures ethical considerations guide our pursuits and that the values of community extend beyond planetary boundaries.

In conclusion, the question of cosmic solitude or community invites us to navigate the intricate tapestry of existence as we envision our future among the stars. As we aspire to harness stellar energies, we also find ourselves at a philosophical crossroads: contemplating how our technological ambitions align with the principles of kinship, responsibility, and ethical stewardship. The quest for Dyson Spheres ultimately teaches us that while we may reach for the cosmos, it is our connections to one another—that deep human fabric of empathy and understanding—that will define who we become in our celestial journey. Through this reflection, we may inspire a vision of humanity that transcends isolation, embracing the interconnectedness that ties us to all beings, terrestrial and extraterrestrial alike.

7.3. Breaking the Barriers of Humanism

As humanity stands on the brink of unprecedented technological advancement, the creation and potential implementation of constructs like the Dyson Sphere compel us to reevaluate the very essence of humanism. Traditionally centered on the dignity, human values, and the potential for improvement of the human condition, humanism encourages exploration and understanding within the constraints of our terrestrial existence. However, the pursuit of megastructures capable of harnessing the energy of an entire star invites us to consider what it means to transcend these boundaries, leading to discussions surrounding post-humanism and the evolution of our societal paradigms.

The emergence of post-humanism, an intellectual movement that questions the limitations of the human experience, flows naturally from the contemplation of Dyson Spheres. By pushing the envelope of technological feasibility, we begin to confront our understanding of life, intelligence, and existence itself. Such advancements encourage the exploration of enhanced bodily capabilities through technology, artificial intelligence integration, and the potential for life beyond Earth. In this sense, post-humanism becomes an avenue through which we can frame our aspirations for the future and the possibilities that lie in our capacity to redesign not only the fabric of society but also the very nature of humanity itself.

With the successful construction of a Dyson Sphere, the relationships between human beings and technology would likely shift radically. Energy abundance would diminish competition for resources, potentially reshaping our socio-political structures toward cooperation and global interdependence. In this post-humanist scenario, we may witness the emergence of a new society where technology becomes an extension of human capabilities, enhancing our cognitive abilities and sensory perceptions. Instead of existing as separate entities, humans and technology could interact symbiotically, resulting in a metamorphosis of consciousness and societal dynamics where the implications of energy use would be radically redefined.

Moreover, as we seek to construct such megastructures, the very notion of progress undergoes reevaluation. Building a Dyson Sphere would symbolize not only engineering prowess but also a collective acknowledgment of our interconnected existence within the cosmos. Post-humanism blurs the lines between the individual and the collective, suggesting a future where our identities expand to include not just our species but the broader community of life in the universe. This compels us to rethink ethical considerations, responsibilities, and the implications of our actions in a cosmic context, urging us to embody values that guide how we interact with one another, with our environment, and potentially with extraterrestrial intelligences.

The implications of pursuing Dyson Spheres also invite us to address the ethical frameworks necessary to govern such technological advancements. With great power comes tremendous ethical responsibility, and as we break through conventional barriers of humanism, our societies must grapple with the potential ramifications of energy abundance. Questions surrounding access to energy resources, ownership of celestial bodies, and stewardship towards both human and non-human entities will take center stage. Such discussions shall underline the importance of communal governance models that prioritize equity, sustainability, and reciprocal relationships between all forms of life.

In essence, engaging in discussions about post-humanism in relation to Dyson Spheres compels us to explore the breadth of human experience in a cosmological framework. As we strive to reach for the stars, we unearth the complexities of existence, prompting reflections on our roles not just as resource consumers but as conscious stewards of the universe. Drawing on the lessons from our planetary journey, we can cultivate visions for a future where the boundaries of humanism expand to embrace an interconnected cosmos—one where humanity recognizes its place within a greater narrative, striving towards a legacy defined by sustainability, compassion, and an unwavering commitment to coexistence across planetary and cosmic scales.

These evolving perspectives challenge the notion of progress as we know it and prompt profound questions regarding meaning, identity, and purpose in a potentially post-human future. As we venture forth, we are reminded that the path to constructing Dyson Spheres may also guide us toward the doors of self-discovery, inviting us to redefine not only our technological trajectories but the very essence of what it means to be human amidst the stars.

7.4. The Frontier Spirit Reimagined

The notion of a Dyson Sphere embodies a reimagining of the frontier spirit that has characterized human exploration since time immemorial. Traditionally, humankind has venturously pursued the unknown —ranging from the great sea voyages of the Age of Discovery to the monumental expeditions of space travel. Each of these endeavors reflects an intrinsic desire to push beyond visible limits, charting territories that once seemed unreachable. Now, as we stand on the cusp of an era where harnessing the energy of stars may shift from speculative fiction to a plausible reality, the essence of this frontier spirit beckons a new interpretation.

In the past, exploration was often bound to immediate geographical landscapes, defined by the boundaries of the Earth. Human beings navigated oceans and landmasses, driven by a blend of necessity, curiosity, and the unpredictable lure of discovery. Every step taken into uncharted terrains was underscored by a rich tapestry of stories

—tales of triumphs and tribulations that spoke to the resilience and ambitions of the human spirit. Areas explored fostered social, cultural, and economic interactions that reshaped civilizations. The frontier was a metaphor for possibility—a reflection of human tenacity in seeking resources, knowledge, and connection.

As we pivot towards conceptualizing Dyson Spheres and other megastructures, the frontier spirit morphs from purely terrestrial exploration into a cosmic endeavor. The quest for building a Dyson Sphere signifies a leap—a transcending of planetary limits towards an engagement with the vastness of space. In this light, the Dyson Sphere serves not merely as a tool for energy harvesting but as an invitation to redefine the essence of what it means to be explorers in a boundless universe. The stars that once served as points of navigation now hold the promise of hosting life-sustaining energies, urging us to reshape our narratives and cultural exchanges.

To harness the energy of stars implies a radical paradigm shift, expanding the frontiers of human existence beyond our planet. The sphere, enveloping and capturing the light of a star, embodies a profound ambition: to not only survive but to thrive. Engaging in this level of cosmic engineering invites communities across the globe to unite in a common goal—to explore, create, and reap the rewards from the very forces that foster life. With this advancement, we would find ourselves not just as inhabitants of Earth, but stewards of a broader cosmic legacy—powerful custodians driving a mutual journey that traverses beyond planetary confines.

Moreover, the expedition to construct a Dyson Sphere proffers the exciting prospect of fostering international and interstellar collaboration. This endeavor demands concerted efforts and shared resources, suggesting that new frameworks of governance may arise, blending ideologies, technologies, and cultures into a cooperative strength capable of undertaking such ambitious projects. Embracing the frontier spirit, societies could cultivate inclusivity and transparency, merging scientific inquiry with artistic expression, ethical deliberation, and political discourse.

Yet, with immense possibilities emerge complex responsibilities. The passing of the torch from earthly exploration to stellar ambitions requires us to confront our intrinsic values and principles amidst grandiose projects. As we look towards the stars with renewed zeal, the essence of the frontier spirit must encompass a commitment to sustainability and ethical stewardship. Harnessing the energy of stars, if done with heedful care and consideration, could unlock a shared narrative—one that emphasizes harmony between technological advancement and the preservation of the celestial environments we seek to engage.

Thus, the frontier spirit reimagined through the lens of Dyson Spheres captures the heart of humanity's aspirations—to reach for the stars while remaining grounded in accountability and respect for universal life. As we prepare to embark on this extraordinary journey, we must remember that our cosmic ambitions are not destined to isolate us in solitude; rather, they can connect us to the greater tapestry of existence, reflecting our collective journey as explorers and custodians of a flourishing universe. Patriating into the uncharted, we may discover that the limits we once knew dissolve amidst the brilliance of the stars, ushering us into a new era defined by vision, unity, and potential.

7.5. Cosmopolitanism: A New Epoch

In an era marked by profound ambition and a longing for connection beyond our earthly realm, the notion of cosmopolitanism emerges as an intriguing concept with implications that extend far beyond the mere gathering of cultures or ideas. As humanity stands on the cusp of potentially transcending its planetary limitations—symbolized by bold ideas like the Dyson Sphere—a new kind of cosmopolitanism begins to take shape, one that unites not just diverse cultures on Earth but also the collective aspirations of intelligent life throughout the cosmos. This evolving paradigm invites profound reflections on our shared existence, interconnectedness, and the responsibilities that come with our newfound capabilities.

The very essence of cosmopolitanism embodies a spirit of inclusivity, emphasizing the recognition of common humanity despite geographical or cultural differences. Traditionally, this perspective has redefined how societies interact, encouraging cross-cultural engagements and collaborations that celebrate diversity and foster understanding. However, as we venture into the grand expanses of space and consider the possibilities of intricate structures like the Dyson Sphere, the conversation surrounding cosmopolitanism expands to encompass not just terrestrial concerns but also the potential for a cosmic community.

Imagine a future wherein advanced civilizations, capable of building Dyson Spheres, engage in dialogues with one another across light-years—a shared endeavor that transcends planetary boundaries and illuminates our collective existence. Such engagement would necessitate new frameworks of communication, ethical considerations, and collaboration that highlight the mutual benefits of energy sharing, knowledge exchange, and technological advancements. In forging these cosmopolitan connections, societies might cultivate a sense of unity not just among their own species but extend this interconnectedness to others that may inhabit the cosmos.

At the core of this evolving cosmopolitanism lies the recognition of our intrinsic shared values as intelligent beings. If Dyson Sphere-like constructs serve as markers of advanced civilizations, the relationships that form between these entities become crucial. The discussions centered around energy cooperation and technological exchange embody a higher ideal—an affirmation that regardless of our origins, our aspirations converge around the pursuit of knowledge and the sustainable coexistence of all life. In pursuing a Cosmic Citizenship ethos, we begin to reshape our identities and responsibilities as stewards of energy, technology, and the planet we call home.

Moreover, the implications of this new cosmopolitanism extend into the discourse concerning ethics and governance. With the potential to wield extraordinary power through the energy harvested from stars, societies must grapple with the ethical dilemmas tied to resource distribution and the repercussions of engaging with other civilizations. The commitment to equitable practices and respectful interactions across planetary systems will be paramount as we strive to avoid the pitfalls of exploitation that marred human history. Developing systems of governance that embody participation, transparency, and shared stewardship will be essential as humanity embarks on this unprecedented cosmic journey.

In contemplating the transition toward this new form of cosmopolitanism, one must also consider how it reshapes our approach to environmental stewardship on a grand scale. As we envision living within a structure capable of solar energy harnessing, our role expands to encompass a deeper consciousness surrounding our responsibility to protect both our home planet and any celestial ecosystems we may encounter. The pursuit of Dyson Spheres should reflect not only our aspirations for progress but also an enduring commitment to ecological preservation and the health of our universal environment.

As we engage in envisioning a future governed by this new cosmopolitanism, the narratives we craft—through art, literature, philosophy, and collective action—will play a pivotal role in shaping our ethical frameworks and guiding principles. This creative and reflective discourse must center on unity, compassion, and respect for life in all its forms—both familiar and foreign. By fostering empathy and cross-cultural understanding, we can facilitate global and interstellar dialogues that honor diverse perspectives while working collaboratively toward shared goals.

In this reimagined epoch of cosmopolitanism, Dyson Spheres may serve not only as beacons of technological achievement but also as symbols for humanity's readiness to embrace its greater responsibilities within the cosmos. We are called to reshape our identities into that of Cosmic Citizens, recognizing the shared essence that links all intelligent life, whatever its origin may be. As we advance technologically and culturally toward this new horizon, let us carry forward our commitment to unity, sustainability, and ethical stewardship, enabling a harmonious existence amidst the cosmic tapestry we collectively inhabit. Ultimately, the journey toward this new epoch of cosmopolitanism, intrinsically linked to the promise represented by Dyson Spheres, is both a profound opportunity and a necessary invitation for humanity to embrace its place among the stars.

8. Dimensional Transitions: Space and Time

8.1. Conceptualizing Scale

Throughout our exploration of the universe, the concept of scale has been pivotal in shaping our understanding of both cosmic structures and our aspirations as a civilization. Dyson Spheres, theoretical colossal constructs intended to capture the energy output of stars, serve as fascinations that compel us to reassess our grasp of scale—an understanding that transcends mere dimensions and enters the realm of existential significance.

First, consider the sheer magnitude of constructing a Dyson Sphere. The mathematics behind such an undertaking is breathtaking, as it would require the assembly of vast arrays of materials, potentially sourced from multiple celestial bodies, to create a structure that could encircle an entire star. This is not merely a matter of engineering logistics but extends to calculations that involve the gravitational dynamics of a system, the thermal energy received from the star, and the distribution of collected energy across potentially vast distances. Each of these considerations illustrates a scale that dwarfs our earthly constructs and challenges our technological and intellectual capabilities.

The concept of scale in relation to Dyson Spheres also begs a reevaluation of our place within the universe. For centuries, humanity has viewed itself as the center of its cosmic narrative—an Earth-centric perspective rooted deeply in our cultural and technological heritage. However, as we contemplate the realities of a Dyson Sphere, we transition from a local understanding to one that necessitates a broader perspective—suggesting that our endeavors must align not only with our ambitions but with a universal context that acknowledges larger cosmic forces at play. Dyson Spheres symbolize the potential for civilizations to ascend to unprecedented evolutionary heights, which shifts our understanding of civilization's capabilities and responsibilities on a galactic scale.

Moreover, the implications of constructing a Dyson Sphere extend into the temporal dimension. We must recognize that such a megastructure would exist over timeframes that vastly exceed human history. The challenges surrounding the sustainability of resources, the long-term governance of energy distribution, and the ecological impacts all point to a need for a longitudinal view on civilization. How do we ensure that our ambitions align with the ecological balance of countless systems and that the energy captured continues to serve future generations? This inquiry forces us to probe the ethical dimensions of intergenerational stewardship and prioritizes sustainability in our technological pursuits.

Furthermore, the construction of a Dyson Sphere may catalyze shifts in cultural narratives and philosophical perspectives within civilizations. Engaging with such ambitious projects would inevitably invoke a reimagining of identity—one that integrates technological prowess while honoring our responsibilities to the universe and acknowledging the potential existence of intelligent life elsewhere. Dyson Spheres may symbolize a quest for enlightenment, igniting reflections on how civilizations navigate their collective paths amid the complexities and expansiveness of the cosmos.

What is more, the act of building and living with a Dyson Sphere invites metaphysical inquiries about being itself. If humanity, or other civilizations, can master the art of energy collection from a star, what does that signify about our relation to life and our existence in the universe? Does the ability to construct such monumental structures enhance our consciousness or change our relationship to divinity? Each of these questions unravels an underlying tapestry of thought that enables us to conceptualize our existence on interstellar scales, promoting a deeper understanding of what it means to explore and contemplate beyond the confines of our planet.

Finally, the interplay between scale and our pursuit of Dyson Sphere technologies encourages a union of scientific inquiry and philosophical reflection. This synthesis positions us to engage with the universe more holistically, capable of considering not only the dimensions of our constructs but the ethical implications, sustainable practices, and shared responsibilities that arise from our journeys into the cosmos. As we contemplate the monumental scale of projects like Dyson Spheres, we embrace a narrative that transcends mere numbers, intertwining the existential with the empirical—a shared human journey that aspires toward not just survival but flourishing within the boundless expanse of the universe.

8.2. Temporal Impacts on Civilization

Throughout the annals of human history, our relationship with time has continuously evolved, intricately linked to our burgeoning understanding of the cosmos. As we contemplate the implications of constructing a Dyson Sphere—an awe-inspiring megastructure designed to harness the total energy output of a star—we must also consider the profound temporal impacts on civilization such a venture would precipitate. The conceptualization of time in the context of a Dyson Sphere presents us with unique challenges and reflections that could redefine our societal structures, cultural narratives, and even our philosophical understandings of existence.

Envisioning a future where Dyson Spheres exist compels us to rethink the very manner in which we perceive and measure time. Traditionally, humanity has understood time as linear: a sequence of events unfolding in a straight line, marked by clocks and calendars that govern our daily lives. Yet, the construction and operation of a Dyson Sphere could lead to a perception of time that is more cyclical, influenced by the rhythms of energy harnessing and the physical interactions between celestial bodies. If we were to encapsulate a star, the relationships between energy collection, conversion, and consumption might forge new models for timekeeping—ones not based solely on the sun's rising and setting, but rather on the complex systems feeding off the star's radiant output.

The essence of a Dyson Sphere might prompt the establishment of novel calendars shaped by the energy cycles harnessed from celestial bodies. In this new temporal framework, communities residing within or connected to a Dyson Sphere would organize their lives around the ebb and flow of star-derived energy—not just in terms of its availability but also as a means of reflecting on their interdependencies with larger cosmic phenomena. These evolving calendars could resonate with the natural rhythms of the universe, deepening humanity's connection to the cosmos and emphasizing the intertwining of celestial and terrestrial existence.

However, as we engage with these tantalizing possibilities, we must also grapple with the complexities of time consistency across various scales. The relativistic effects stemming from the immense mass and energy manipulation inherent in a Dyson Sphere could introduce fascinating shifts in the perception of time. As we approach the gravitational thresholds imposed by such colossal constructs, the theoretical implications of time dilation might become pronounced. Phenomena described by Einstein's theory of relativity suggest that individuals engaging with significant gravitational influences may experience time differently than those in less intense fields. Thus, the very nature of 'simultaneity' could be altered, leading to profound sociocultural implications as communities navigate different temporal experiences.

Imagine a scenario wherein some citizens experience "real" time at a slower rate while embedded within the gravitational influences of a Dyson Sphere, while others living further away perceive time at the typical rate. Such discrepancies might manifest as social fragmentation—frictions arising from an inability to synchronize moments, plans, or events across the micro-communities formed both in-space and on Earth. This could lead to an intriguing exploration of social conventions surrounding birthdays, celebrations, and memorials—initiating customs that reflect the unique temporal experiences across various proximities to the Dyson Sphere.

Moreover, the philosophical implications of time within the context of a Dyson Sphere evoke existential inquiries about our existence. If our perception of time could shift dramatically due to the influences of a megastructure, what would it mean for humanity's sense of legacy and continuity? Traditionally, we have grasped time as the chronicler of our stories—the moments threading together the tapestry of our existence. Introducing new notions of time, possibly predicated on energy cycles or relativistic effects, invites us to ponder if our memories, histories, and identities could similarly evolve in response.

Thus, as we consider the temporal impacts of a Dyson Sphere on civilization, we hone in on the intersections of science, philosophy, and culture. We invite dialogue that challenges our understanding of time as fixed, exploring not just its measurements but its meaning. How will these reimagined perceptions change how we construct our narratives, make commitments to one another, and foster connections across generations and cosmic expanses?

At the heart of these temporal reflections lies an opportunity for humanity to redefine itself amid the vast cosmic backdrop. By inviting new ways of thinking about time, we allow ourselves to embrace the possibilities of collaboration, innovation, and unity in a universe that beckons us forward. Through our engagement with ambitious projects like Dyson Spheres, we may cultivate a profound sensual acknowledgment of our existence and interconnectedness within the unfolding chronicle of creation—a narrative that transcends the limitations of our earthly confines and ventures boldly into the cosmic unknown. In essence, as we journey towards the stars, we reaffirm our commitment not merely to harness energies but to reflect upon the very foundations of existence that bind us all in this ever-expanding tapestry of time.

8.3. Astrophysical Consequences

The concept of astrophysical consequences primarily addresses the significant impact that the construction and operation of megastructures like Dyson Spheres would have on the surrounding cosmic environment. In this context, we delve into the intricate interplay of gravitational dynamics, energy manipulation, and the broader implications for celestial bodies and possibly life itself.

At the heart of the astrophysical consequences of a Dyson Sphere lies the gravitational interplay between the megastructure and the star it envelops, as well as any nearby celestial objects. A Dyson Sphere, particularly in its more realistic incarnation as a Dyson Swarm, would likely consist of numerous individual satellites or energy-collecting platforms. Each of these components would exert gravitational forces on one another and on the central star, which could lead to noteworthy shifts in the orbits of planets and other celestial bodies.

For instance, the gravitational effects of a Dyson construct may alter the stability of planetary orbits within the solar system. If the structure captures a significant portion of the star's energy output, thereby impacting solar radiation levels and altering the dynamics of energy dispersal throughout the system, the environmental conditions on nearby planets could change dramatically. Such alterations might bring about advancements or setbacks in the evolution of life, affecting climate patterns, gravitational balance, and potentially fostering new ecosystems.

Moreover, constructing a Dyson Sphere could introduce complex orbital mechanics into the system. The requirement for these components to operate efficiently while maintaining stable orbits around the star calls for intricate calculations to prevent collisions and gravitational interference. These calculations would need to account for potential perturbative forces from planets, moons, and asteroids, ensuring that energy-harvesting satellites remain in designated zones without compromising the equilibrium of the complete solar system.

In addition, there is the question of how the vast amount of energy captured by a Dyson Sphere would be managed and utilized. The energy harnessed could be transmitted not only to other structures within the Dyson Sphere but also back to the home planet or neighboring celestial bodies. The implications for solar system dynamics include alterations to electromagnetic fields, potential radiation effects, and consequences for any life that could exist or is nurtured within these regions.

The operation of a Dyson Sphere and its impact on the dynamics of space would also raise questions about the long-term sustainability of such megastructures. Would the gravitational effects be fully understood and manageable? Or might they lead to unintended consequences such as destabilizing orbits of planets or causing asteroid pathways to change, potentially impacting the delicate balance of existing lifeworlds?

Beyond the immediate astrophysical concerns, the consequential impacts may resonate across a broader cosmic perspective. For example, if humanity or another advanced civilization succeeds in constructing a Dyson Sphere with visible consequences—such as substantial manipulation of stellar energy—it could serve as a detectable signature to other civilizations. This raises exciting yet sobering notions about how civilizations potentially signal their presence in the cosmos while unveiling questions surrounding the responsibilities adhered to by any civilization capable of such feats.

As we proceed to conceptualize and evaluate the repercussions of Dyson Spheres and similar constructs, we must engage in a multidimensional understanding of the universe—a universe that operates under laws of physics that are both predictable and full of nuance. Factor in the combination of gravitational dynamics, energy manipulation, and the possible repercussions on surrounding celestial bodies, and we find ourselves at the threshold of profound astrophysical inquiries—questions that not only challenge our empirical knowledge but also tease our imaginative wanderings about life, civilization, and our place in the universe.

In summary, the astrophysical consequences of Dyson Spheres extend beyond mere energy harvesting; they embody a comprehensive tapestry of gravitational interplay, energy dynamics, environmental shifts, and potential interstellar communications. By exploring these consequences, we delve deeper into the essence of what it means to be a civilization on the brink of profound change—challenging us to reconcile our ambitions for cosmic engineering with an unwavering commitment to sustainable practices, ecological balance, and our responsibilities across the cosmic spectrum. Ultimately, such inquiries will shape our narrative as we reach outward toward the stars and embrace the intricacies of the universe as both architects and stewards of our collective destiny.

8.4. Time Dilation and Timekeeping

In the exploration of time's nature, the theoretical Dyson Sphere invites a profound reconsideration of our understanding of timekeeping and dilation as it relates to cosmic engineering. Situated within the framework of stellar energy capture, the very concept of a Dyson Sphere implies significant interactions with the fundamental forces of astrophysics, consequently affecting how we measure, perceive, and experience time.

Imagine a civilization that embarks on the construction of a Dyson Sphere, enveloping a star and harnessing its abundant energy. As the structure becomes operational, the sheer scale and mass of such a construct could imply gravitational effects significant enough to induce changes in the flow of time—an attribute well-documented in the theory of relativity. According to Einstein's theories, time is not a constant; it can flow differently depending on the gravitational fields surrounding an object and relative velocities. Thus, the accumulated mass of a Dyson Sphere—even if constituted of dispersed satellites or panels—could create localized distortions in spacetime, resulting in time dilation effects.

Specifically, those positioned closer to the Dyson Sphere, especially in regions experiencing intense gravitational fields near the star, might encounter a considerably slower passage of time relative to observers situated farther away, perhaps on Earth or other celestial bodies. This discrepancy would lead to fascinating sociocultural implications for the civilization utilizing the Dyson Sphere's energy. Individuals drawn towards the gravity well might perceive time differently, raising intricate questions about societal cohesion. Would they maintain contact with more distantly situated populations? How might life events—like aging, achievements, or milestones—be linked across temporally disparate zones?

Given such an environment, our traditional methods of timekeeping would need a substantial revision. Clocks based on Earth's rotation or vibrations could become impractical; new temporal frameworks must emerge that accommodate varying timeflows dictated by gravitational variance. Timekeeping systems might evolve to synchronize experiences across the spectrum of gravitational forces influencing each community. Understanding these variations would require substantial advancements in technology, further emphasizing the necessity for collaboration across this newly reimagined society.

As we ingrain these ideas into our narratives about Dyson Spheres, it's also essential to reflect philosophically on time's nature itself—how our conception of linearity and permanence is inevitably shaped by our lived experiences and the environments around us. In an expansive Dyson Sphere scenario, our reliance on terrestrial anchors for measuring time could shift, leading to a deeper understanding of cyclical phenomena and cosmic alignments as vital contextualizations for planetary and interstellar lives.

Moreover, as humans venture into constructing and utilizing Dyson Spheres, effectively managing the time dilation effects becomes more than just a technical challenge; it opens doors to a wealth of existential inquiries regarding identity and continuity. Bridging temporally disparate communities may foster new dialogic cultural exchanges, philosophies, and worldviews—reflecting our profound adaptability in the face of cosmic realities.

Timekeeping, in this light, transcends its conventional boundaries. The implications of building a Dyson Sphere not only reshape how we measure time but also challenge our perspectives on life's rhythms and the nature of existence itself. It invites us to consider time as a malleable, interconnected tapestry—a fundamental aspect of humanity's journey amongst the stars. In this context, we find ourselves at the intersection of technology, philosophy, and experience, urging us to navigate the complexities of time as we embark on this cosmic odyssey.

Through these reflections, we are reminded that our relationship with time is not fixed but fluid—a mirror reflecting humanity's potential as we engage with the profound possibilities represented by Dyson Spheres and other future constructs. In moving beyond conventional timekeeping towards a shared cosmic sense of temporal rhythms, we may deepen our understanding of what it means to exist in a universe that constantly unfolds dimensions of wonder and significance beyond our immediate perceptions.

8.5. Gravitational Interplay

Gravitational interplay is a crucial concept in understanding the dynamics that would unfold with the construction and operation of a Dyson Sphere. This colossal structure, designed to encapsulate a star and harness its energy output, would inherently influence the gravitational forces within its solar system, resulting in significant alterations to the orbits and behaviors of surrounding celestial bodies. As we explore the gravitational implications of such a megastructure, we delve into the intricate web of relationships between the stars, planets, and any engineering marvels that might encircle the star.

At the core of the gravitational interplay associated with a Dyson Sphere lies the principle of gravitation itself, which dictates that any massive object exerts a force upon other masses, pulling them toward it. In the case of a Dyson Sphere, the sheer scale of the construct could introduce new gravitational dynamics into the existing solar system. If we imagine a fully realized Dyson Sphere as a rigid shell (albeit a theoretical construct), the force it exerts would interact with the gravitational influences of the star and any planetary bodies nearby. This interaction poses intriguing questions: What gravitational forces would emerge? How would these forces change the trajectories of neighboring planets?

Consider the construction of a Dyson Swarm—a more realistically flexible concept of the original Dyson Sphere proposal. Each satellite or energy-collecting unit would possess its own mass and gravitational field, contributing to the overall dynamics of the environment. As these components orbit around the star, they would alter the gravitational landscape and create new variables for the stability of orbits among planets in the vicinity. Emulating cosmic ballet, the gravitational influences would need to be carefully balanced to maintain stability among celestial bodies, necessitating precise calculations to avoid collisions or erratic orbital paths.

An important facet of this gravitational interplay concerns the influence on planetary orbits. The aggregate mass of the Dyson Swarm surrounding a star would introduce gravitational perturbations that could either stabilize or destabilize the orbits of planets and moons. Depending on the configuration of the Dyson components, the gravitational effects could lead to altered orbits for nearby planets. For instance, an influx of additional mass in the vicinity of a gas giant could change the configuration of its moons or pull smaller celestial bodies into new trajectories, potentially resulting in collision courses or impact events.

The existence of a Dyson Sphere might even alter the star's radiation output as the structure captures and utilizes a portion of this energy. This would mean that planets receiving energy from the star would experience changes in their climates and energy availability. Such a change could affect not only the development of ecosystems but also the potential for life on these planets, compounding the significance of gravitational interplay between the megastructure and surrounding celestial entities.

Moreover, gravitational interactions do not operate in isolation; they interlink with other forces at play in the cosmos. The presence of asteroid belts, comets, and other celestial bodies would also contribute gravitational nuances to the system. The potential existence of a Dyson Sphere could provide a framework for further exploration of resource acquisition from these smaller bodies, as gravitational interactions influence the trajectories of asteroids and other objects navigating the star's influence.

The gravitational interplay surrounding a Dyson Sphere also extends to fundamental inquiries about the energetic balance within the system. The energy harvested from the star would need to simultaneously consider the gravitational forces at work to effectively manage energy transfer. When using electromagnetic systems for energy transmission between satellites or back to planets, engineers would need to factor in the influence of gravitational forces on energy transport mechanisms, ensuring efficient flow without destabilizing orbital relationships.

Additionally, as we engage the concept of a Dyson Sphere with its broader gravitational consequences, we are invited to contemplate philosophical ramifications. The operations and consequences of manipulating gravity could deeply resonate with human understanding of interconnectedness in the cosmos—a realization that our ambitions to harness cosmic energy involve not just bravado but a respect for the delicate balance of celestial existence. As civilizations advance towards the building of a Dyson Sphere or similar constructs, grappling with gravitational interplay urges a profound sense of humility and responsibility—both to our solar system and potentially to other civilizations within our cosmic community.

In conclusion, the gravitational interplay associated with a Dyson Sphere entails a complex amalgamation of forces influencing the stability of celestial orbits, energy dynamics, and potential interactions between various celestial bodies. This gravitational landscape invites scientific, philosophical, and ethical inquiries that not only illuminate our navigational strategies within the cosmos but also impart deeper understandings of the responsibilities inherent in such cosmic engineering. As we proceed on this journey of exploration and harnessing energy from the stars, it becomes imperative to approach our ambitions with consideration for the delicate interplay of forces that govern the universe. Through this lens, we reaffirm our commitment to tread lightly as we reach for the stars, seeking harmony amid the gravitational tides that weave together the cosmic fabric.

9. Fundamentals of Astrobiology and Cosmic Industries

9.1. Defining Astrobiology

Defining astrobiology involves establishing this interdisciplinary field as the scientific study of life in the universe, deeply intertwined with the concepts of life's existence, development, distribution, and the fundamental conditions that make life possible. Astrobiology transcends the limits of Earth and utilizes the full breadth of scientific inquiry, melding aspects of biology, ecology, geology, and planetary science to explore and understand life's potential in diverse environments, especially in relation to hypothetical structures like the Dyson Sphere.

Astrobiology's scope is expansive, encompassing the search for microbial life on Mars, the analysis of extreme environments on Earth, and the characterization of exoplanets located in habitable zones around distant stars. The inquiry begins with fundamental questions: What constitutes life? How did life originate? What are the elemental, atmospheric, and environmental prerequisites for sustaining life? Central to these questions is the understanding of how life processes could adapt to environments vastly different from our own—an important consideration for any discussions on Dyson Spheres, which represent engineering constructs aimed at harnessing stellar energy.

When interpreting the implications of constructing a Dyson Sphere, astrobiology becomes a crucial lens as it informs our understanding of civilizations capable of such monumental feats. The very essence of a Dyson Sphere challenges our perceptions of life and technology, suggesting that advanced civilizations may manipulate their stellar environments to sustain their existence. This concept pushes investigators toward considering not only the infrastructure needed for energy collection but the biospheric implications of such endeavors. As civilizations become adept at energy harvesting, a consequent inquiry arises: How might these advanced life forms evolve, adapt, and interact symbiotically with their environment, and what ethical considerations must accompany such technological mastery?

The role of astrobiology in this context does not merely rest in the speculative domain; it actively shapes our understanding of planetary formation and evolution within diverse galactic ecosystems. Insights gained from researching life in extreme environments on Earth—such as deep-sea hydrothermal vents, acidic lakes, and polar ice caps—offer valuable guidance in anticipating planetary conditions elsewhere. Such knowledge fosters predictions concerning the potential for life to thrive in environments influenced by Dyson-like energy constructs on other worlds.

Additionally, astrobiology delves into identifying biosignatures—chemical indicators of life—in planetary atmospheres. The construction of a Dyson Sphere or its equivalents could yield detectable byproducts, such as artificial atmospheric changes or waste heat signatures that may serve as targets for astrobiological investigation. Searches for extraterrestrial life, particularly in the vicinity of such megastructures, set the stage for examining biospheric dynamics and linking findings back to our understanding of life's adaptability across various magnitudes and contexts.

The ethical dimensions of astrobiology fundamentally intersect with the existential reflections concerning our role as potential architects within the cosmos. The study of life beyond Earth prompts profound considerations about our responsibility toward alien ecosystems, particularly those that may be impacted by our interstellar explorations or manipulation of stellar environments. Should we encounter other advanced civilizations or ecosystems, the lenses of astrobiology offer a moral framework to guide ethical engagement, emphasizing stewardship over exploitation.

Furthermore, the exploration of astrobiology encourages a collaborative dialogue among scientists, ethicists, and communities that transcends the barriers of discipline. As the investigation of life in the universe grows, researchers will increasingly benefit from integrating diverse perspectives and methodologies, nurturing probes into ethical considerations, conservation efforts, and the search for mutual understanding among various life forms, whether discovered on distant exoplanets or constructed through advanced technology like Dyson Spheres.

In conclusion, defining astrobiology within the context of Dyson Spheres and cosmic exploration places it at the forefront of humanity's quest to uncover life's potential in the universe. As we advance our technological capabilities while maintaining ethical responsibility, astrobiology will continue to illuminate the intricacies of life, offering pathways toward sustainable coexistence, mutual understanding, and a richer comprehension of our place within the larger cosmic narrative. Through this integrated approach, we not only seek to understand the life that may exist beyond our home but also deepen our appreciation for the delicate threads connecting all life across the vast tapestry of the universe.

9.2. Interdependencies of Cosmic Technological Ecosystems

The intricate web of cosmic technological ecosystems emphasizes the expansive scope of interdependencies inherent in harnessing star energy. At the center of our exploration lies the theoretical Dyson Sphere—a hypothetical structure designed to encompass a star, capturing its vast energy output and fundamentally transforming the technological landscape of any civilization that constructs it. Understanding the interdependencies within these cosmic systems illuminates how advanced civilizations might navigate the challenges and intricacies of engineering marvels on such an astronomical scale.

Central to the construction and operation of a Dyson Sphere is the web of technologies that must work in concert to ensure its functionality, sustainability, and effectiveness. A plethora of interconnected systems would be necessary, encompassing energy generation, resource management, infrastructure maintenance, and community governance. Each technological facet must be designed to coexist seamlessly, forming a cohesive ecosystem that adapts to the fluctuating demands of both energy demands and celestial interactions.

First and foremost, energy generation emerges as the linchpin within this technological ecosystem. The process of capturing and converting stellar energy involves sophisticated materials science, advanced photovoltaics, and energy transmission systems that collectively ensure maximized energy yield. As the Dyson Sphere harvests energy from the star, real-time monitoring systems would be required to assess energy output and optimize collection methods. This necessitates coupling with data analytics and artificial intelligence, enabling predictive modeling that adjusts energy collection strategies based on solar activity and celestial phenomena.

Moreover, the integration of robotics and automation becomes crucial for the ongoing maintenance of the Dyson Sphere and surrounding infrastructure. Advanced robotic systems will perform routine inspections, repairs, and real-time adjustments in response to any changes in the structural integrity of energy-collecting satellites or components. This autonomy allows for a minimum reliance on human operators, especially in potentially hazardous environments prevalent within space. The interplay between robotics and real-time data collected by an interconnected sensor network ensures the longevity of the Dyson Sphere, facilitating adaptive responses to unforeseen challenges and promoting resilience in an ever-evolving cosmic context.

The resource management component embodies another layer of interdependency within the technological ecosystem. Building a Dyson Sphere would necessitate materials sourced from various celestial bodies—asteroids, moons, and possibly nearby planets. Thus, efficient transportation systems must be intricately designed to ensure seamless retrieval and conveyance of materials. This might involve the development of advanced spacecraft, autonomous mining operations, and resource allocation systems that prioritize ecological sustainability and minimize disruption to the target environments.

An equally essential aspect of this technological tapestry is the governance model established to oversee energy distribution and usage. As energy abundance generated by the Dyson Sphere reshapes societal structures, the focus will shift towards collaborative governance frameworks that promote equity and sustainability. The communities residing in close proximity to the Dyson Sphere may require representatives who engage in collective decision-making, reflecting the values and needs of a diverse populace. Open dialogues, ethical guidelines, and transparent processes will serve as cornerstones within this governance system, ensuring that the immense power derived from stellar energy fosters cooperation rather than division.

Simultaneously, the interdependencies across cosmic technological ecosystems extend beyond mere hardware and energy systems, weaving interconnected narratives surrounding societal evolution and cultural identity. As advanced civilizations engage with the challenges surrounding the Dyson Sphere's construction and operation, the prevailing philosophical frameworks guiding human pursuits must be re-evaluated. The promotion of a collective consciousness that emphasizes stewardship, sustainability, and cosmic interconnection becomes vital as civilizations transition from terrestrial existence to thriving within a sprawling stellar community.

In essence, the interdependencies of cosmic technological ecosystems reflect the nuanced interplay of engineering, science, ethics, and community engagement. As we delve further into the theoretical implications of constructing Dyson Spheres, we recognize that these monumental achievements extend beyond energy production, catalyzing societal transformations, philosophical inquiries, and new ways of relating to both the cosmos and each other. By weaving a coherent narrative of interdependence, we embrace the ambitious dream of reaching for stellar energies while grounding ourselves in principles that guide our journey as responsible stewards of the universe.

9.3. In Search of Life Beyond Sol

The quest for life beyond the confines of our solar system has become a driving force in astrobiology, particularly as researchers explore the implications of constructing colossal structures like Dyson Spheres. These hypothetical megastructures, designed to harvest the energy output of stars, not only provoke our imaginations but also challenge our understanding of the conditions under which life might exist elsewhere in the universe. As humanity reaches ever closer to mastering advanced technologies, the search for life beyond Sol takes on new dimensions, not merely as an academic pursuit but as an integral part of our cosmic narrative.

Central to the exploration of life beyond our solar system is the understanding of the conditions hypothesized to support life. The ecological niches that can sustain biochemical processes essential to living organisms are as varied as the worlds they inhabit. The inquiry begins with identifying locations where simple microbial life might thrive, looking into exoplanets located in habitable zones around distant stars. Here, astrobiologues utilize models that rely on knowledge gained from extremophiles—microorganisms on Earth capable of surviving extreme conditions—to guide their search for similar environments in the cosmos.

However, the implications of a Dyson Sphere extend far beyond detecting microbial life; they compel us to investigate the potential for advanced extraterrestrial civilizations. If any civilization reaches the technological sophistication required to create such a monumental structure, they would be leveraging energy on a scale unimaginable to humanity today. The existence of a Dyson Sphere could serve as a beacon to attract our attention, resonating with seekers of advanced intelligence. As theorists postulate, the infrared signatures emitted by massive energy harvesters might be detectable from light-years away, prompting scientific investigations into their origins.

The search for life in the context of a Dyson Sphere intertwines with the ethical dilemmas posed by humanity's role within the cosmic order. Encounters with advanced civilizations capable of creating such constructs raise complex questions surrounding communication, cultural exchange, and moral responsibilities. If the quest for life leads us to regions of the universe populated by intelligent species, our approach must be informed by the principles of mutual respect and reciprocity. The landscapes of astrobiology will require an examination of how to navigate potential interactions in a manner that honors the dignity of all forms of life, fostering a spirit of collaboration rather than conquest.

Another essential aspect of our search lies in the potential for discovering remnants of past civilizations. As we expand our observational capabilities, we may unearth evidence of construction projects on distant exoplanets, relics of technological legacies forged by civilizations that perhaps peaked long ago. The ramifications of encountering evidence of these bygone societies can reshape our understanding of technological evolution, recognizing that the path from primitive to advanced life is not linear and that civilizations may experience stagnation or collapse as they grapple with their own existential dilemmas.

Moreover, as we pursue our search for life beyond our solar system, it becomes crucial to reflect on the interdependencies inherent in our quest. The conceptualization of Dyson Spheres as potential indicators of intelligent life not only enhances our scientific endeavors but also calls for a harmonized approach to exploration—all while maintaining a deeply-ingrained respect for the unknown. The ethical frameworks guiding this search must prioritize the preservation and protection of ecosystems and the potential for biocompatibility among diverse life forms.

In summary, the endeavor of searching for life beyond Sol, particularly in the context of Dyson Spheres, invites us to profoundly engage with our existence. It compels us to expand our understanding of what life might be, how civilizations could evolve, and what ethical considerations must guide our engagements with any intelligent species we encounter. As we nurture these inquiries, we remain mindful of the wondrous potential that awaits us among the stars, an exploration that intertwines our ambitions with profound philosophical reflections on our shared journey as stewards of the cosmos.

9.4. Astrobiology's Ethical Expansion

Astrobiology has always been an intersection of imagination and scientific inquiry. Through this lens, the ethical expansion of astrobiology in the context of advanced structures like the Dyson Sphere challenges us to rethink our relationship with life in the universe—specifically, how we consider the existence of other sentient beings and the ramifications of encountering their technologies.

At the core of this ethical expansion lies the necessity to acknowledge the potential presence of other intelligent civilizations that might be constructing—or have constructed—Dyson Spheres and similar megastructures. The reality that these civilizations could manipulate cosmic energy raises profound questions regarding the nature of their existence, their values, and the implications of their technological evolution. If humanity aspires to ascend to the cosmic heights represented by Dyson Spheres, we must also grapple with responsibilities that come with an understanding of our place in the broader universe.

The first ethical consideration relates to the very definition of 'life' and 'intelligence.' As we explore possibilities of encountering alien civilizations with advanced technologies, we will likely need to broaden our understanding of what constitutes life. The implications of discovering life that experiences reality in ways starkly different from ours might compel us to embrace the idea of multiple intelligences, each with its interpretations of existence and ethics. This diversity necessitates an ethical framework that respects both the sovereignty and existential narratives of any civilization we encounter.

Moreover, the existence of Dyson Sphere-like constructs, particularly those visible from a distance through altered energy signatures, could prompt a sense of responsibility in our observations. As stewards of our own planet and potential interstellar citizens, we must maintain ethical considerations regarding our interactions. How might our quest for knowledge and discovery affect civilizations engaged in their cosmic narrative? Approaching these questions with sensitivity and humility can shape our responses, ensuring we do not impose our desires or values on others.

Additionally, if entities capable of constructing Dyson Spheres exist, we must consider the ethical implications of potentially interfering with their habitats. Our explorations may leave footprints that disrupt delicate extraterrestrial ecosystems, undermining their existences. The ethical imperative to tread lightly echoes throughout historical narratives of colonization on Earth; it serves as a reminder that encounters with other civilizations must be marked by respect, cooperation, and a commitment to understanding their unique ecological contexts.

The speculative nature of Dyson Spheres invites us to reflect not just on what we might learn from other intelligent beings but also what responsibilities arise from our potentially shared technological evolutions. If we are to encounter alien civilizations, we must be prepared for dialogue—a reciprocal exchange of knowledge, culture, and ethical considerations that honors the diversity of life that may exist beyond our solar system. This dynamic encompasses understanding the challenges faced by these civilizations, fostering relationships founded on empathy and mutual respect.

Moreover, in our quest for Dyson Sphere technology, we must ensure that our explorations are driven by aspirations for peaceful coexistence, environmental sustainability, and social responsibility. Engaging with astrobiology's ethical expansion creates a framework that encourages humanity to embrace its collaborative nature, urging us to become custodians of life in all its forms. By fostering values that extend beyond narrow self-interests, we can nurture compassion and interconnectedness, allowing for the possibility of thriving together in a cosmos filled with potential.

Ultimately, the ethical expansion of astrobiology in the context of Dyson Spheres challenges humanity to redefine its cosmic narrative. As we contemplate our aspirations to harness the energy of stars, we must engage with the broader consequences of our ventures. This entails not only an acknowledgment of the advanced civilizations we may encounter but also a deepened commitment to ethical principles that prioritize respect, equity, and sustainability. Through this lens, astrobiology evolves into an exploration of our place in the tapestry of existence—where the ambitions of advanced engineering must resonate with an enduring ethic of care and responsibility for all life across the cosmos.

9.5. Stimulating Galactic Economies

The concept of stimulating galactic economies within the context of Dyson Sphere technology invites us to envision an intricate interplay of energy production, technological innovation, and societal transformation. As civilizations evolve towards the engineering of such monumental constructs capable of capturing the vast energy output of stars, a range of economic opportunities would emerge, fundamentally reshaping interaction patterns not just within a single solar system but potentially across vast expanses of space.

At the heart of this exploration lies the vast potential for energy resources. A fully operational Dyson Sphere would harness an almost inexhaustible supply of stellar energy, shifting from localized scales of energy consumption to a galactic framework. This transition could stimulate a cosmic economy where energy scarcity—a dominant factor in human socio-economic structures—becomes a relic of the past. In such a context, the sheer abundance of energy could pave the way for industrial expansions, enhanced scientific research endeavors, and advanced interstellar travel capabilities, establishing a new socioeconomic order defined by energy-rich interdependent communities.

As energy becomes plentiful through Dyson Sphere technology, the implications extend beyond energy production alone. The ability to generate and distribute vast quantities of energy would likely catalyze advancements in technology and infrastructure, leading to the creation of a wider array of technological tools, applications, and enterprises. Industries might evolve that specialize in energy management, storage technologies, and energy-efficient systems, propelling society into a new epoch of innovation. New markets and job opportunities tied to energy-related technologies would emerge, echoing the transformative economic shifts observed throughout human history during industrial revolutions.

Moreover, this paradigm shift could stimulate a re-envisioning of societal interactions on a cosmic scale. The establishment of energy availability as a common resource would likely encourage cooperative governance models among different celestial communities. Collaboration in sharing energy sources, technology, and knowledge might become the foundation for politically organized alliances that span across solar systems, creating new forms of governance that prioritize sustainability and mutual support over competition. The investment in interstellar relationships cultivated through energy trade would foster a robust galactic economy, stimulating cultural exchanges and enhancing global cooperation among species capable of cosmologically significant engineering.

The economic implications of Dyson Sphere technology probably also encompass enhancements in transportation and travel. As energy becomes abundant, propulsion systems designed to explore other planets and systems would likely become more efficient and accessible. This capacity could stimulate industries centered on space tourism, resource extraction, and research missions, creating a new frontier for economic growth. As humanity reaches outwards, the natural interstellar connections would integrate knowledge, resources, and culture from diverse civilizations, amplifying the economic impacts across the cosmos significantly.

However, as invigorating as these potentials are, they also bring forth a multitude of ethical considerations as societies step into a galactic economy powered by Dyson Sphere technology. With energy abundance comes the responsibility of ensuring that this resource is utilized sustainably and equitably, fostering a culture committed to collective well-being. The construction of governance systems that create fair access and management of resources becomes critical to prevent the rise of inequalities stemming from energy ownership or technological disparity.

One must consider the long-term environmental impacts of this new economic reality as well. The insights derived from astrobiology remind us of the interconnectedness of life across celestial systems, raising questions about the stewardship of energy resources that transcend planets and stars. Ensuring that the pursuit of energy does not come at the expense of ecological degradation in both artificial and natural environments must be foundational in guiding galactic economic development.

In conclusion, the stimulating of galactic economies through Dyson Sphere technology positions humanity at the precipice of transformative change. From addressing energy scarcity and empowering technological innovation to promoting cooperative interstellar relationships, the implications ripple through societal structures, ethical frameworks, and ecological considerations. As we dare to imagine a future where Dyson Spheres become operational, we are invited to craft a narrative that harmonizes our technological ambitions with our responsibilities to the cosmos and its diverse inhabitants. In doing so, we affirm our role as stewards of energy and life, intertwining our destinies amid the cosmic tapestry that beckons us to explore.

10. Songs of the Celestial Spheres: Music and Mathematics

10.1. Harmonizing Mathematics

If we are to harmonize mathematics with humanity's quest for the stars, the intricate relationship between mathematical principles and the cosmos reveals profound truths about both our universe and our aspirations within it. Mathematics serves as both a language and a framework through which we interpret the laws governing energy, structures, and interactions in our celestial surroundings. In the context of constructing and operating a Dyson Sphere, this framework becomes not merely a toolkit for architects and engineers but a lens through which we perceive our existence in a boundless universe.

To begin this exploration, it is imperative to appreciate the mathematical foundations that underpin the concept of a Dyson Sphere itself. The idea of surrounding a star to capture its energy output is deeply rooted in principles of geometry and calculus. The calculation of the surface area, volume, and the energy dynamics of the star necessitates a precise mathematical approach, ensuring that every detail is meticulously accounted for. For instance, determining the optimal distance at which to place energy-collecting satellites, while accounting for gravitational forces, intricacies of solar radiation, and energy efficiency, relies heavily on equations that govern orbital mechanics.

As we extend beyond mere calculations, mathematics encapsulates a broader cosmic harmony that resonates throughout the universe. The laws of physics, which are fundamentally described in mathematical terms, demonstrate elegant symmetries and patterns that govern everything from the smallest particles to the largest structures in the cosmos. The Fibonacci sequence and the golden ratio, for example, appear in natural formations, harmonizing our understanding of beauty, growth, and organization. Within the realm of a Dyson Sphere, recognizing such mathematical symmetries opens avenues for designing structures that do not only function effectively but resonate aesthetically and harmoniously with the universal principles around us.

This exploration reveals the notion that Dyson Spheres represent more than just a solution to energy needs; they become symbols of our quest to harmonize with the cosmic symphony. The pursuit of such grand engineering feats requires interdisciplinary collaboration —bridging disciplines such as physics, mathematics, engineering, and the arts. As each field contributes to the endeavor of building Dyson-like constructs, we assimilate diverse perspectives that enrich our understanding of existence itself, fostering a holistic approach worthy of the monumental challenges ahead.

In contemplating the harmonic relationship between mathematics and the cosmos, it becomes apparent that music emerges as a profound metaphor connecting both realms. The mathematical principles that underpin the frequencies and resonances of sound are directly tied to the patterns found in light and energy, representing a universal language that transcends individual experiences. As cosmic engineers imagine the profound wonders of a Dyson Sphere, music becomes a parallel expression of our aspirations—a way to evoke emotion and connection while bridging the gap between the tangible and the abstract.

The act of conceptualizing and constructing megastructures evokes hymns of creativity and innovation, awakening a collective chorus that resonates throughout the community of humankind and any intelligent life that may share our universe. Music inspired by the cosmos calls upon composers and artists to craft works that embody the awe and mystery of celestial wonders, from symphonies that mimic the rhythms of orbiting planets to electronic compositions that simulate the pulsing energy of a star. These artistic expressions serve to unify disparate cultures under common themes of exploration and ambition—harmonizing our dreams into movements that echo across the galaxy.

Ultimately, the harmonization of mathematics with the ambitious quest represented by Dyson Spheres speaks to our collective potential. It reaffirms that by engaging deeply with the mathematical symphonies of the universe, we can craft narratives and technologies that elevate our understanding of existence. In doing so, we forge pathways that not only lead us to sustainable energy but also illuminate the infinite possibilities awaiting us among the stars—where every calculation, mathematical truth, and creative expression become notes in an intricate cosmic score, echoing through time as we journey forth into the boundless expanse. As we embrace this intertwining of mathematics, music, and the cosmos, we are reminded that our aspirations can lead to harmony, discovery, and, ultimately, a profound connection with the universe itself.

10.2. Music Inspired by the Cosmos

Music has always held a special place in humanity's exploration of the universe, serving as a bridge between our experiences and the vast, often inscrutable cosmos. As we contemplate the theoretical construct of a Dyson Sphere—an immense structure designed to harness the energy of a star—music inspired by the cosmos takes on a unique significance. It encapsulates the emotions, possibilities, and philosophical inquiries that arise as we venture beyond the confines of our planet.

Artistic works drawn from cosmic inspirations often reflect the awe and wonder of the universe, inviting us to experience the beauty of celestial events and the mysteries that lie beyond our reach. Composers like Gustav Holst, with his renowned suite "The Planets," captured the grandeur of our solar system through music, evoking the personality of each planet as if they were sentient beings. This piece serves as a precursor to the musical explorations sparked by the idea of Dyson Spheres; it evokes questions of existence, identity, and our place in the boundless expanse of space.

As artists grapple with these themes, contemporary compositions reminiscent of these vast structures weave a narrative that transcends mere sound. The works of modern composers and electronic musicians use synthesized sounds and orchestral arrangements to create rich auditory landscapes that mirror cosmic phenomena. From the rhythmic pulse of celestial orbits to the harmonics of stellar explosions, musicians channel the essence of the cosmos into their craft, creating a sense of connection that resonates deeply within the human spirit.

Many artists find inspiration in the concept of a Dyson Sphere itself, feeding off its underlying principles to craft pieces that metaphorically explore the potential of harnessing stellar energy. These musical interpretations provide a canvas for creative expression, allowing listeners to explore notions of energy, ambition, and the intricacies of life as they relate to the act of reaching for the stars. Such compositions often invite their audiences to envision the vastness of the cosmos, immersing them into a soundscape that reflects the awe-inspiring engineering feats that humanity aspires to achieve.

The interplay between music and technology also runs deep in the discussions surrounding cosmic engineering. The advancements in sound technology not only enable the creation of innovative compositions but also evoke the harmony between life and technology. Electronic music, by drawing on sophisticated technological techniques, serves as a modern soundtrack to our quest for greater connectivity with the universe. These compositions can resonate with the vibrational energies that composers aim to capture—a profound reflection of the potential synthesis of life and technological innovation encapsulated in the idea of a Dyson Sphere.

Beyond the specific properties of musical pieces, the universality of language and sound plays a crucial role in how music inspired by the cosmos communicates its messages. The innate human response to music transcends cultural boundaries and connects us intimately to shared emotions and visions. As we consider possibilities like the Dyson Sphere, we begin to imagine how music can shift from a terrestrial experience to a universal one, embodying an expression of what it means to reach out into the cosmos.

In essence, the pursuit of Dyson Spheres and the accompanying artistic reflections embody an invitation to reflect on our shared humanity, the yearning for exploration, and the mystical energies that bind us to the universe. As we dance between science and art, mathematics and music, we are reminded that our ambitions to dwell among the stars are woven together in a narrative that speaks to the aspirations of life itself—infinitely intertwined with the rhythms and resonances of existence beyond our planet.

As we compose the musical legacy of our exploration, we grasp the ethereal threads that connect us to the cosmos—a reminder that our songs today are echoes of tomorrow's universe, reverberating through the vast, dark sea of space as we continue our journey into the unknown. Whether through symphonies, electronic soundscapes, or improvisational performances, the celebration of our celestial ambitions resonates beyond words, leaving lasting imprints of human creativity that reflect the dream of thriving amidst the stars.

10.3. Vibrations of Life and Technology

In this subchapter, we delve into the intricate interplay between life and technology within the context of Dyson Spheres, exploring the profound implications these colossal megastructures might have not only on our quest for energy but also on the evolution of civilization itself. The analogy of "vibrations" serves as both a metaphor and a tangible representation of how these constructs could facilitate communication and interactions among diverse forms of life across the cosmos.

The concept of Dyson Spheres embodies the duality of human ambition and technological prowess. At the core of their design lies an intricate understanding of physics, mathematics, and engineering, reflecting our collective knowledge and ingenuity. As we contemplate the construction of such vast structures, we are reminded that these advancements are not simply calculated feats of engineering but also resonate with the vibrational essence of life throughout the universe.

The vibrations of life can be interpreted in multiple dimensions; they encompass the fundamental energies that sustain ecosystems on Earth and beyond, as well as the cultural and emotional expressions that unite us as sentient beings. A Dyson Sphere, designed to encircle a star and harvest its energy output, would not merely serve as a mechanical entity; it could emerge as a symbol of interconnectedness —an embodiment of our aspirations to harmonize technology with ecological balance.

As we embark on constructing a Dyson Sphere, we must also consider the vibrations of technology, the rhythms associated with advanced machinery, robotics, and self-regulating systems that will govern the functioning of these ambitious projects. The integration of automation and artificial intelligence within the ecosystem of a Dyson Sphere could lead to intricate technological symphonies—machines designed not only for labor but also for cooperation and adaptability. These systems might utilize real-time data analytics to enhance their operations, learning from their environment and making decisions that optimize energy collection while minimizing ecological disturbances.

However, as we advance in our mastery of technology, the vibrations of life compel us to examine the ethical implications and responsibilities tied to our endeavors. The construction of a Dyson Sphere invites questions about stewardship—how do we ensure that our pursuit of energy wealth does not come at the expense of surrounding ecosystems or the potential life forms that might inhabit those environments? The harmonization of technological ambitions with ethical considerations forms an intricate melody, guiding us toward sustainable practices that honor the interconnectedness of all existence.

When we consider the vibrations of life and technology as they converge within the context of Dyson Spheres, we are also prompted to engage with the universality of language and sound. Just as music transcends cultural boundaries, the pursuit of stellar energy and the dream of building a Dyson Sphere could inspire a shared cosmic language among intelligent beings. The potential discovery of advanced civilizations capable of creating similar constructs emphasizes the possibility of collaborative dialogues between species that may employ unique forms of communication rooted in their technological advancements.

This intersection of life and technology fosters imaginative inquiries into how cultures express their identities amidst the grand scales of energy harvesting and cosmic exploration. It invites us to envision scenarios where diverse civilizations exchange knowledge and stories through the vibrations resonating from their experiences, fostering a sense of communal connection that transcends planetary and galactic distances.

In the quest for energy through Dyson Spheres, we recognize that our technological pursuits are woven intricately with the underlying vibrations of existence. As we reach for the stars, the echoes of our aspirations remind us that the journey is not solely about harnessing energy but also about understanding our place within the tapestry of life. The vibrations of life and technology urge us to embrace our roles as stewards of cosmic energy, awakening to the harmonies that connect us all within the expansive universe, as we endeavor to build bridges of understanding and cooperation among the stars.

Through this lens, we see Dyson Spheres not only as fantastic constructs of advanced technology but as profound symbols of our collective aspirations—an emblem of how life and technology can harmoniously coexist, creating new possibilities for collaboration, understanding, and sustainable existence across the cosmos.

10.4. Universality of Language and Sound

In the realm of astrobiology, the search for life beyond Earth intertwines intricately with the concept of constructible megastructures such as the Dyson Sphere. This hypothetical structure, meant to garner the entirety of a star's output, fosters deep reflections on the potential for life elsewhere in the universe. As we consider the implications of such a monumental undertaking, we are prompted to explore not only the biological prerequisites for life but also the complex relationship between advanced civilizations and their environments.

Astrobiology seeks to answer fundamental questions about life's existence, its development and the conditions under which it thrives. With the potential for a Dyson Sphere, the inquiry expands to include the implications of technology and energy management within a cosmic framework. The study of extremophiles on Earth—organisms that inhabit extreme conditions—provides insight into possible forms of life that might adapt to environments surrounding other stars. As we refine our understanding of astrobiology, we recognize that the fundamental characteristics that allow life to flourish are not limited to Earth, shaping our predictions about the diversity of life throughout the cosmos.

Moreover, the construction of a Dyson Sphere may signal the existence of advanced extraterrestrial civilizations adept at manipulating and harnessing cosmic energy. These societies would not merely survive—they would thrive in their environments, actively molding them for their purposes. The implications of a Dyson Sphere as an energy-collecting entity invite us to consider the sustainability of such technologies. How would civilizations balance their technological advancements with environmental stewardship, ensuring that their manipulation of celestial bodies does not disrupt the delicate ecosystems surrounding them?

As we engage with the potential existence of other intelligent civilizations, astrobiology unfolds complex ethical considerations surrounding our responsibilities as cosmic explorers. The mere prospect of encountering advanced societies capable of constructing Dyson-like structures necessitates a rigorous examination of our ethical frameworks. Upon discovering such civilizations, what guiding principles will inform how we interact with them? How do we ensure mutual respect while recognizing the unique narratives of other life forms?

The potential discovery of remnants of ancient astrobiological civilizations could further enrich our understanding of technological evolution in the universe. If such entities constructed megastructures and advanced technologies, they may leave behind traces that provide insights into their values, ambitions, and technological trajectories. Investigating remnants or signals from long-gone civilizations may unveil the cyclical nature of progress and destruction, reminding us of the importance of preserving our resources and ethical commitments as we endeavor to venture among the stars.

In summary, the exploration of astrobiology within the context of Dyson Spheres expands our inquiry into the nature of life, technology, and our responsibilities. As we gaze into the cosmos, our pursuit of knowledge is complemented by a deepened understanding of our shared existence—one that beckons us to approach it with humility and respect. Ultimately, the journey toward constructing Dyson Spheres and uncovering the mysteries of life beyond our solar system embodies our innate quest to understand not only the universe but also ourselves as a species ambitious enough to explore the stars.

10.5. Ephemeral Echoes of Eternity

The threads of speculation intertwine seamlessly with scientific inquiry as we delve into the subchapter titled "Ephemeral Echoes of Eternity." As we examine the concept of a Dyson Sphere, we find ourselves contemplating the vast expanse of the cosmos and our ephemeral existence within it. Throughout human history, music has served as a bridge, a universal language that resonates with our deepest emotions and connects us to both the finite and infinite. The echoes of our aspirations, fears, and dreams reverberate through melodies crafted by our ancestors and contemporary musicians alike, inviting us to explore the relationship between our human experience and the cosmos.

At its core, the Dyson Sphere symbolizes the pinnacle of human ambition—an audacious endeavor to harness the energy of an entire star. Such a monumental construction inspires us to reflect on the nature of existence and the interconnectedness of life in the universe. It highlights the paradox of our existence: we are but transient beings on a tiny planet, yet we strive to reach the stars and understand their mysteries. This quest is mirrored in the timeless art of music, echoing our desires to explore, connect, and transcend our limitations.

Music, with its ability to evoke emotion and capture the essence of life, serves as a powerful vessel through which we interpret the cosmos. Composers like Gustav Holst in "The Planets" have harnessed the awe inspired by celestial bodies, weaving complex harmonies that resonate with the grandeur of the universe. In this spirit, a Dyson Sphere becomes a metaphor for the harmony we seek—a symbol of how humanity's technical prowess can coexist with our artistic aspirations, blending the concepts of engineering and artistic expression into a cohesive vision.

As we imagine the construction of a Dyson Sphere, we also contemplate the profound implications of such an undertaking for our understanding of music and creativity. The very act of constructing a megastructure around a star—a structure that could capture its light and shine energy throughout a civilization—presents opportunities to explore soundscapes as expressions of technological and cultural identity. The vibrations produced by the processes of energy harvesting, transformed into musical compositions, could convey the experience of living within or alongside such structures.

This synergy between life and technology, captured through music, reminds us that our aspirations are fundamentally linked to our emotional experiences. By fostering a culture that embraces artistic expression alongside scientific pursuits, we cultivate a society that sees beyond the confines of mere survival and embraces the beauty of creation. In understanding the whispers of the stars, we not only connect with our celestial surroundings, but we also harmonize our identities, redefining what it means to be stewards of the cosmos.

In contemplating the ephemeral nature of human existence contrasted with the potential for eternal echoes of our creations, we recognize the legacy we leave behind. Should we realize the construction of a Dyson Sphere, it would echo the triumph of human ingenuity—a testament to our aspirations and an expression of our understanding of the universe. This legacy—as transient as life itself—invites us to engage with the cosmos thoughtfully and sustainably, ensuring that our contributions enrich the tapestry of existence.

In essence, the notion of "ephemeral echoes" invites us to reflect on how our journey through the stars intertwines with the very fabric of life itself. As we strive to master the technologies that allow us to capture stellar energy, we must also navigate the complexities of our interconnectedness, fostering cultural growth alongside technological advancement. The harmonization of these elements reaffirms our commitment to creativity, exploration, and a sustainable future as we heed the call of the cosmos.

The pursuit of a Dyson Sphere represents not just the mechanics of energy harvesting but also the music that resonates in the hearts and souls of all beings. It reflects an eternal dance of ambition, creativity, and the ephemeral nature of existence—an ongoing symphony written in the stars as we seek to leave our mark on the canvas of the universe.

11. Engineering for the Stars: Essential Technologies

11.1. Nanotechnology in Space

As humanity strives to explore the vast cosmos, the applications of nanotechnology emerge as pivotal in the construction, maintenance, and operational efficiency of massive megastructures like the Dyson Sphere. This remarkable advancement offers a new frontier in engineering, intertwining the worlds of miniature engineering solutions with bold architectural ambitions on an astronomical scale.

At the core of nanotechnology's significance in space exploration is its ability to innovate and optimize materials at an unprecedented scale. Through the manipulation of materials at the atomic or molecular level, nanotechnology allows for the creation of components that are not only lightweight and durable but also capable of withstanding the extreme conditions of space. Components for a Dyson Sphere, such as solar panels and structural supports, can be engineered using nanomaterials designed for maximum efficiency and resilience. These materials could demonstrate properties like increased flexibility, advanced thermal management, and enhanced energy absorption capabilities—essential traits for devices exposed to the harshness of interstellar environments.

Additionally, the convergence of nanotechnology with other fields of science introduces new possibilities for self-assembling structures. In a Dyson Sphere scenario, nanobots—tiny robotic devices engineered at the nanoscale—could be deployed to autonomously construct solar-collecting satellites or to conduct repairs on existing structures. These autonomous nanobots could operate on the principles of swarming behavior, mimicking natural processes found in insects or microorganisms. They would work collaboratively to form complex structures and respond adaptively to their environments, ensuring that the Dyson Sphere remains efficient and functional over extensive periods.

The utilization of nanotechnology also extends to energy delivery and management. A Dyson Sphere's operation hinges on the effective transmission of energy harvested from a star to the various points of use, whether on neighboring planets or within space habitats. Advancements in nanoscale materials could lead to the development of highly efficient energy storage systems, enabling the creation of superconducting cables that minimize energy loss during transmission. Such innovations would empower civilizations to harness and distribute stellar energy equitably and sustainably.

Another remarkable application of nanotechnology lies in environmental monitoring systems embedded within the Dyson Sphere ecosystem. Nanosensors can be deployed to assess the structural integrity of the megastructure, monitor temperature fluctuations, and measure radiation levels. These nanosensors would operate in real-time, feeding data to centralized control systems that could autonomously adjust operations or initiate repairs, enhancing safety and effectiveness.

Furthermore, the applications of nanotechnology could influence the approach to resource acquisition. Whether mining asteroid belts for materials or deploying resource-gathering systems on terrestrial planets, employing nanoscale devices can increase efficiency and reduce waste. For example, nanotechnology could enable selective mining processes that extract only the necessary materials while preserving the surrounding ecosystems, aligning with principles of sustainability and ecological stewardship.

However, with these remarkable technological advancements come ethical considerations that require careful deliberation. As we embrace the potential of nanotechnologies in the realm of megastructures, we must also contemplate the implications of deploying devices capable of autonomous action on celestial scales. The ability to manipulate materials at the nanoscale raises questions about the extent of control we should exert over our environments and the life forms that may inhabit them.

In this context, the integration of nanotechnology within Dyson Sphere construction introduces a rich tapestry of possibilities for engineering, energy management, and environmental interactions. As civilizations push the boundaries of space development, realizing the full capabilities of nanotechnology becomes integral to constructing resilient, sustainable cosmic architectures that echo our technical prowess and environmental consciousness. Balancing these remarkable advancements with a deep respect for the celestial ecosystems we engage with will ultimately define humanity's legacy in the pursuit of cosmic energy, reconciling ambition with responsibility in the grand narrative of existence.

In conclusion, nanotechnology serves as a cornerstone in the quest to construct and operate Dyson-like megastructures, offering solutions that are lightweight, efficient, and autonomous. It intertwines with the aspirations of advanced civilizations to engage with the cosmos sustainably while raising essential questions about ethics and environmental stewardship. As we look toward a future intertwined with nanotechnology, we must embrace not only our technical capabilities but also our role as custodians of life and resources in the vast universe. This journey toward harnessing stellar energy through ingenious applications of nanotechnology will echo through the vast tapestry of time, forging a new chapter in our collective existence as we soar alongside the stars.

11.2. Automation and Robotics

The advent of automation and robotics in the context of Dyson Sphere construction signifies a monumental leap in both technological capability and conceptual ingenuity. As humanity stands on the brink of potentially realizing such ambitious megastructures, the role of advanced automation and robotic systems emerges as a critical linchpin in the engineering, operational maintenance, and sustainability of these colossal entities. These advancements not only promise efficiency and precision but also redefine how civilizations approach complex engineering challenges in an environment as unforgiving and vast as space.

At the core of this discussion lies the necessity for scalability and efficiency in executing the various phases of Dyson Sphere construction. An undertaking of this magnitude would typically exceed the limits of human labor alone; thus, the deployment of automated systems becomes essential. Robotics enables the assembly of countless components needed—all elements that would form an intricate lattice of energy-collecting units encircling the star. Utilizing autonomous robots to fabricate, transport, and position these units significantly accelerates the construction timeline while mitigating potential risks associated with human involvement in remote and hazardous environments.

Automation in this context encompasses a variety of systems—from lightweight drones capable of navigating within the stellar environment to heavy-duty construction bots engineered to withstand extreme temperatures and the vacuum of space. These robotic units can execute intricate tasks with impressive precision, adhering to pre-programmed designs while adapting to unforeseen challenges encountered during the construction phase. With advanced machine learning algorithms, these robots could optimize operations in real time based on environmental feedback—adjusting placement or construction techniques to enhance stability and efficiency.

Furthermore, once the Dyson Sphere is operational, the role of robotics extends beyond construction into continuous maintenance and adaptation. As celestial bodies frequently experience unpredictable interactions—such as solar flare activity or micrometeoroid impacts—having a fleet of autonomous robots designated for routine inspections and repairs is indispensable. These self-regulating systems could operate independently, equipped with tools and sensors designed to assess structural integrity and ensure that energy-collecting units function optimally over decades, if not centuries.

Automation also promotes the transition towards a sustainable approach to operating a Dyson Sphere. The energy output harnessed from the star can facilitate the power required to operate these robotic systems, creating a feedback loop of energy utilization that reduces reliance on external resources from Earth. With robotics operating autonomously, the management of resources becomes inherently more efficient, signaling a shift toward a model of interstellar engineering that prioritizes ecological balance and sustainability.

The synergy between automation and human oversight also raises profound questions about the human role within these systems. As robotic systems take on greater responsibilities, the nature of human employment, interaction, and oversight would need re-evaluation. A society capable of constructing a Dyson Sphere would likely emphasize collaboration between human intuition and robotic efficiency, fostering a partnership that not only improves operational outcomes but also encourages innovation in machine-human interactions.

Moreover, the implications of advanced automation and robotics extend into cultural spheres, redefining our understanding of creativity and ingenuity. The potential for autonomous systems to contribute to the design and optimization of such structures inspires philosophical discourse on the nature of creation. Are these constructs merely reflections of human design, or do they also embody a form of creativity authored by intelligent machines? The expanding capabilities of robots could prompt new ways of thinking about authorship and the merging of technology with the artistic pursuit of cosmic engineering.

In conclusion, the integration of automation and robotics into the discourse surrounding Dyson Sphere construction not only enhances practical engineering approaches but also paves the way for a reimagined future where civilizations blend human intellect with advanced technological systems. As we navigate the complexities of this brave new world, we embrace the prospect of harnessing stellar energy with a focus on efficiency, sustainability, and mutual advancement —ensuring that the quest for Dyson Spheres remains a symbol of hope bound in the intricate dance between life and technology in the universe.

In exploring how advanced propulsion systems underpin the theoretical undertakings of Dyson Sphere projects, we find ourselves confronting revolutionary possibilities that could transcend current technological limitations. The quest to harness the energy output of an entire star intuitively requires the development of propulsion technologies capable of supporting such monumental constructions —an endeavor that demands innovative engineering and deep understanding of fundamental physics.

The first consideration in this domain centers on the limitations of existing propulsion technologies. Conventional rockets, with their reliance on chemical combustion, possess finite thrust capabilities and limited ranges, rendering them inadequate for building and transporting the necessary materials to construct a Dyson Sphere, particularly in locations far beyond our current reach. Consequently, advanced propulsion systems must pivot away from these conventional methods and explore alternative technologies that can provide sustainable, high-efficiency solutions for interstellar travel and construction.

One promising avenue is nuclear propulsion systems, which can produce thrust without relying solely on chemical reactions. Nuclear thermal propulsion, utilizing a nuclear reactor to heat propellant gases, offers potentially significant increases in specific impulse— a key performance metric for propulsion systems. This transition represents a pivotal step toward establishing transportation capabilities that can support the logistics of Dyson Sphere construction, ushering in an era defined by more robust access to materials sourced from the asteroid belt and potentially even other planets.

Another promising candidate is ion propulsion technology, which uses electric fields to accelerate ions and produce thrust—an approach known for its high efficiency and prolonged operational duration. While ion engines currently do not provide the immediate power necessary for liftoff from Earth, they excel during long-duration space missions. This method is particularly attractive for transporting materials once positioned in space, where its efficiency can be maximized, ensuring that the complex logistics of Dyson Sphere assembly become feasible over extended timelines.

Electric propulsion can also be expanded into concepts like electro-magnetic sails (em-sails) or laser propulsion systems. An em-sail, which utilizes solar or planetary radiation pressure, can harness energy from the sun and navigate without traditional propellant. However, while this method may be ideal for gradual travel across solar systems, it must be examined closely in conjunction with energy generation and transmission for Dyson Sphere projects.

Laser propulsion systems represent another exciting frontier for potential development. Here, ground-based or space-based lasers would direct energy towards light sails mounted on spacecraft, facilitating high-thrust acceleration without the mass penalties associated with traditional propellants. In constructing a Dyson Sphere, laser propulsion could enable rapid transportation of construction materials between celestial bodies while ensuring energy-efficient means of navigating through our solar system and beyond.

Furthermore, the exploration of advanced propulsion systems encompasses not just the mechanics of travel but also speaks to the evolution of societal paradigms surrounding exploration and resource utilization. Understanding the challenges tied to interstellar logistics will push civilizations to innovate crossing not only technical barriers but also social ones, emphasizing collaborative efforts, shared responsibilities, and cultural exchange.

The challenges and discoveries surrounding advanced propulsion systems thus form a vital foundation of the Dyson Sphere narrative, interlinking bold engineering projects with a reimagined understanding of human aspirations in traversing the cosmos. As civilizations steer towards these innovations, they recognize that the quest for harnessing salvaged energies should inherently reflect values of progress, cooperation, and sustainability—principles that uphold our standing as responsible explorers seeking a harmonious existence with the universe.

In summary, propulsion systems capable of realizing Dyson Sphere projects must evolve away from conventional propulsion methods toward advanced technologies that amplify efficiency, range, and sustainability. By exploring nuclear, ion, laser, and electromagnetic propulsion methodologies, we forge new paths toward interstellar travel, thereby expanding our capabilities and aspirations as we continue our quest to harness the energy of stars and explore the intricate tapestry of existence among the celestial wonders.

As we wade into the interplay between quantum mechanics and macroengineering, fascinating dimensions of theoretical concepts emerge—particularly in the context of constructing monumental structures like Dyson Spheres. The principles of quantum mechanics, which govern the behavior of particles at the smallest scales, can yield innovative insights into how large-scale engineering projects might be conceived, designed, and constructed, bridging the realms of the infinitesimal with the cosmic.

Quantum mechanics introduces us to the idea of superposition, entangled states, and wave-particle duality, challenging our understanding of physical interactions. Paradoxically, while we typically conceive of macroengineering projects through deterministic frameworks, quantum phenomena suggest that uncertainty and probability also play vital roles in shaping our realities. As we extend these principles to the potential of a Dyson Sphere, we can envision new methodologies that leverage quantum effects to impact materials, propulsion, information transfer, and even sustainability.

One area where quantum mechanics may influence Dyson Sphere projects is in the development of new materials with extraordinary properties. The manipulation of atomic structures through quantum principles can lead to revolutionary advancements such as superconductors that operate at higher temperatures or metamaterials capable of harnessing and redirecting electromagnetic waves. These materials —not constrained by traditional limitations—could form the backbone of energy-collecting components, paving the way for designs that maximize efficiency and minimize losses.

In exploring the principles of entanglement, we also uncover intriguing possibilities for information transmission across the Dyson Sphere infrastructure. Quantum communication systems, leveraging the phenomenon of instant correlations between entangled particles, could facilitate secure and instantaneous data transfer among the myriad of autonomous systems responsible for monitoring and managing the energy collection process. This would be particularly essential in maintaining the integrity of operations and the stability of interdependent systems within a Dyson Sphere environment.

As we envision the operation of a Dyson Sphere, the implications of quantum mechanics urge us to rethink traditional engineering paradigms. Rather than approaching challenges with a purely macroscopic perspective, we rediscover the interconnectedness that quantum principles elucidate—the notion that systems are not isolated but inherently linked. This recognition fosters a collaborative culture among scientists, engineers, and ethicists tasked with realizing the construction and operation of a Dyson Sphere.

However, the integration of quantum mechanics also prompts critical, reflective inquiries into the ethical dimensions of manipulating matter at such fundamental scales. As civilizations harness these technologies, responsibilities accompany the potential for unintended consequences arising from quantum manipulations. We must grapple with the implications of wielding such power and how it might influence our broader understanding of existence in the cosmos.

In conclusion, the intersection of quantum mechanics with the ambitious pursuits of macroengineering, particularly in the context of Dyson Spheres, opens pathways to innovative solutions and visionary projects that transcend our current frameworks. By embracing the probabilistic nature of quantum phenomena, we enhance our understanding of large-scale constructs while acknowledging the ethical responsibilities tied to these advancements. As we pursue the potential of coupling quantum principles with macroengineering, we reaffirm our commitment to harmonizing technology with cosmic stewardship, ensuring a sustainable and interconnected existence in a universe that beckons us to explore.

As we delve into the significance of self-regulating systems in ensuring the resilience and sustainability of Dyson Spheres, we uncover a compelling narrative that embodies our aspirations to engage intelligently with the cosmos. The successful operation of a Dyson Sphere demands more than mere engineering feats; it requires thoughtful integration of autonomous systems, advanced technologies, and robust governance that can respond dynamically to the challenges within the celestial environment.

Self-regulating systems encompass a variety of technologies designed to operate without constant human intervention, prioritizing adaptability and efficiency. In the context of a Dyson Sphere, these systems would likely monitor a multitude of parameters— from energy levels and structural integrity to environmental factors such as radiation exposure and proximity to other celestial bodies. By employing real-time data analysis, predictive algorithms, and machine learning, self-regulating systems can autonomously manage the infrastructure, enabling it to respond fluidly to changing conditions while optimizing energy collection and distribution.

One of the core advantages of self-regulating systems lies in their ability to ensure ongoing adaptation and resilience amid potential challenges. For example, the dynamic environment surrounding a star may subject a Dyson Sphere to fluctuations ranging from solar flares to micrometeoroid impacts. Equipped with adaptive responses, these autonomous systems can quickly assess threats and take corrective actions—redirecting energy collection mechanisms, reinforcing structural supports, or initiating repairs—all without necessitating human oversight. This not only enhances the longevity of the megastructure but also reduces vulnerabilities associated with human error.

Moreover, the integration of self-regulating systems can foster a culture of sustainability in the management of resources. As energy is harvested from stellar output, these systems could also optimize energy distribution across connected colonies or planets. For instance, they can prioritize energy allocation for essential services, monitoring consumption patterns and ensuring that excess energy is stored or redirected appropriately. This dynamic balancing of energy consumption exemplifies a commitment to efficient resource management, echoing principles of ecological stewardship vital in a cosmic context.

Beyond technical and operational considerations, the implementation of self-regulating systems strains our understanding of the human role within this technological landscape. As machines take on greater decision-making responsibilities, society must rethink its relationships with automation. The relationship between humankind and its creations may evolve from direct control to collaborative partnerships, where humans guide the overarching ethical considerations while robocrafts provide executional capacity. This shift emphasizes the need for continuous dialogue around human-machine interactions, ensuring that ethical implications remain at the forefront of any operational framework.

It is worth considering how these autonomous systems influence the cultural narrative surrounding Dyson Sphere construction. The narratives we craft about living alongside advanced technologies will shape societal values, influence educational frameworks, and redefine our approaches toward innovation. The potential emergence of a society that collaborates with intelligent self-regulating systems encourages an exploration of identities—prompting reflections about what it means to be human in an age increasingly intertwined with automation and artificial intelligence.

In conclusion, the inclusion of self-regulating systems as essential features in Dyson Sphere operations highlights our pursuit of adaptability, resilience, and sustainability within cosmic engineering. These autonomous technologies enable efficient management of resources and contribute significantly to the longevity of such structures— embodying the aspiration to harmonize technology and ecological stewardship. As we navigate this transformative journey toward harnessing stellar energies, we affirm our commitment to understanding the interplay between humans and machines, ensuring that our quest echoes with ethical considerations that leave a profound impact on our shared cosmic narrative.

As we return our focus to the intricacies of alien societies and their relationship with technological evolution, one discovers a plethora of opportunities and challenges that arise from advanced constructs such as Dyson Spheres. The potential for civilizations to harness stellar energies inevitably leaves behind markers that signal their advancement, drawing interest from humanity as we probe the cosmos for signs of intelligent life.

Indicators of advanced civilizations capable of constructing Dyson Spheres encompass a range of detectable signatures, from modifications noted in stellar luminosity to thermal emissions captured by infrared observatories. For instance, Dyson proposed that a civilization capable of erecting such megastructures would likely generate excessive heat as a byproduct of energy collection. This thermal signature could serve as one of many vital clues in the Search for Extraterrestrial Intelligence (SETI) as we seek out anomalous emissions that suggest artificial constructs orbiting distant stars.

Moreover, such advanced civilizations may exhibit other phenomena observable from afar. For example, variations in light intensity from a star coupled with unexpected periodic dimming could indicate the presence of satellites harvesting energy. Following the case of KIC 8462852, where uncharacteristic dimming led to speculation about extraterrestrial megastructures, scientists remain vigilant for similar anomalies occurring in stellar observations. These investigations help spur discussions on the potential existence of Dyson Sphere-like constructs, framing a narrative that bridges astronomical observation with the search for life beyond Earth.

Theoretical frameworks for alien technologies can expand our understanding of what civilizations could achieve with their knowledge of physics, resource utilization, and energy management. Assuming that these cultures have reached the threshold of constructing Dyson

Spheres, one would expect to discover technological advancements that challenge our existing paradigms. Speculative scenarios may explore quantum communications, advanced materials with robust integral properties, or even propulsion technologies that enable interstellar travel, reshaping our comprehension of what forms of life could thrive in distant star systems.

In light of these considerations, the encounter with extraterrestrial megastructures also raises profound questions about cultural exchange across light-years. How would humans interact with intelligent beings capable of constructing enormous energy-collecting entities? What ethical frameworks would guide dialogues and collaborations with such civilizations? Mutual respect and acknowledgment of diverse values become paramount as we seek to foster meaningful connections that transcend cultural barriers.

Such frameworks will also compel us to consider not just direct interactions between civilizations but the broader implications for technological evolution. Recognizing the lessons drawn from encounters may add dimensions to our societal narratives—inviting shifts in how we perceive civilization's artistic pursuits, environmental stewardship, and ambitions to explore the cosmos.

Lastly, the complexities of ethical concerns when contemplating interstellar interactions require careful deliberation. The potential for cultural misunderstanding, conflict, or imposition when engaging with more technologically advanced societies raises essential inquiries regarding the responsibility of advanced civilizations to treat newly discovered forms of intelligent life with dignity and respect. Guidance from philosophical traditions and interdisciplinary dialogue will be instrumental along this journey, helping us cultivate ethics that promote collaboration rather than dominance in encounters with life among the stars.

In summary, the indicators of advanced civilizations and their technological evolution shape the discourse surrounding Dyson Sphere constructs, inviting humanity to explore the cosmos with an inquisitive spirit. As we investigate these signals from distant stars, we expand our comprehension of life, technology, and the ethical responsibilities inherent in our quest. Through this exploration, we not only chart potential paths forward for humanity but also embrace the understanding that we are part of a vibrant tapestry, woven together with the myriad threads of life across the cosmos as we endeavor to reach the stars together.

As we contemplate the future of technological evolution in perspective of alien societies, we open doors to profound discussions regarding cultural exchanges across light years. The quest for advanced megastructures, such as Dyson Spheres, beckons a thorough investigation into how societies might engage in communication and collaboration within the vastness of the cosmos. In seeking to understand these dynamics, we highlight the opportunities and challenges that emerge from interstellar connections—guiding us to consider what it means to be members of a broader cosmic community.

One of the foundational aspects of these exchanges centers on shared aspirations between civilizations equipped with advanced technologies. If we uncover evidence of extraterrestrial societies capable of constructing Dyson Spheres, this revelation could inspire a new chapter in cosmic dialogue—one rooted in mutual understanding, respect, and cooperation. These civilizations, having achieved mastery over immense energy systems, would present opportunities for collaboration that extend beyond simple technological exchanges.

However, the act of connecting across light years requires careful navigation of cultural differences, ethical frameworks, and potential misunderstandings. Every society's values, histories, and technological approaches inform its perspective and methods of interaction. As we endeavor to engage with other civilizations, we must cultivate awareness and appreciation for their unique narratives, fostering dialogues that transcend language and communication barriers.

In practical terms, establishing effective communication principles across civilizations becomes imperative. The universality of mathematics, sound, and music may serve as vital bridges between disparate cultures—providing common ground for sharing knowledge, values, and aspirations. By embracing these elements, advanced civilizations could craft a language of exchange that honors both their individuality and interdependence.

However, cultural exchanges extend beyond discussions of technology; they encompass ethical considerations regarding resource management and ecological sustainability. The knowledge gained from engaging with civilizations that harness stellar energy may illuminate new pathways towards governance, environmental stewardship, and shared responsibilities. Such collaborations could yield new solutions to our contemporary challenges, enabling advancements in sustainable practices—promoting mutual benefit for all parties involved.

The complexities of potential disparities in technology would naturally inform dialogues and ethical frameworks surrounding cultural exchanges. Advanced technologies may create imbalances in power dynamics—raising questions about equity, fairness, and potential exploitation. Navigating these nuances will require consideration of principles that prioritize reciprocal relationships and mutual respect among civilizations.

Therefore, as we imagine the potential scenarios surrounding cultural exchange across galaxies, we are prompted to reflect on our own responsibilities as ambassadors to the cosmos. The realization of Dyson Sphere technology carries with it not only the empowerment to harness incredible energy but also the moral obligation to approach newfound connections with humility and empathy. Ensuring that dialogues are imbued with cultural sensitivity becomes essential, fostering relationships that honor the dignity of all sentient beings engaged in this remarkable cosmic narrative.

In summary, cultural exchanges across light years present a formidable and transformative opportunity for humanity in the age of Dyson Spheres. The potential for collaboration fosters whispers of hope, suggesting that interstellar communication may extend our understanding of life and technology while threading together the rich tapestry of existence. This journey invites us to invest in a future where we embrace shared aspirations while navigating the complexities of cosmic diversity, ultimately seeking harmonious coexistence among intelligent beings across the universe.

As we delve further into the ethical considerations arising from potential interactions with technologically superior civilizations, the discourse surrounding Dyson Spheres sheds light on the responsibilities that accompany such advancements. The prospect of encountering alien societies capable of constructing colossal megastructures evokes deep reflections about our moral obligations, the principles of equity, and the ethics of coexistence with potentially intelligent life beyond our own.

Primarily, one of the most pressing ethical concerns hinges on the balance of power. If humanity were to encounter a civilization distinguished by its ability to construct Dyson Spheres, we must address how to engage with such beings in ways that promote mutual respect, shared interests, and equitable exchanges. The potential for an imbalance of power could lead to exploitation, manipulation, or imposition of values, which highlights the need for establishing ethical frameworks that prioritize fairness, understanding, and cooperation.

Moreover, the ethical implications entwined with resource management become particularly pertinent in discussions surrounding Dyson Sphere technologies. The decision-making processes regarding energy utilization and distribution must be approached with awareness and caution, recognizing that disparities may arise when advanced civilizations control unprecedented energy resources. Should negotiations occur between societies with varying levels of technological development, ethical frameworks must ensure that agreements respect the rights and interests of all parties involved, mitigating the potential for conflict while fostering symbiotic relationships.

Another ethical concern dovetails with the potential ecological impacts that could arise from interspecies interactions. As we explore Dyson Sphere technologies, we must grapple with how these constructs affect surrounding ecosystems and the potential life forms inhabiting them. If encountering other civilizations that utilize megastructures, we are confronted with questions regarding our responsibilities towards their environments. Navigating the intricacies of ecological ethics becomes key to ensuring that our actions promote preservation over exploitation, creating a paradigm in which we safeguard the sanctity of diverse life throughout the cosmos.

Furthermore, the delineation of ethical principles in interstellar contexts extends to the subject of communication. Should contact be established, mutual understanding and respect become paramount in facilitating productive dialogues between civilizations. The balance of knowledge sharing requires sensitivity to cultural nuances, historical contexts, and philosophical beliefs that have shaped other societies' interpretations of existence and technological advancements. Appraising our dialogues through an ethical lens ensures that interactions inspire cooperation rather than undermine the core values of those with whom we engage.

As we explore the narratives surrounding Dyson Spheres and the potential for encounters with other advanced societies, we confront ethical questions that guide our endeavors in the cosmos. The principles we establish and uphold will reflect our shared humanity and the values we choose to embody as we step into the vast expanse of interstellar exploration. A commitment to ethical stewardship provides not only a moral compass but also a foundation for building authentic relationships that respect the dignity of all intelligent beings.

In conclusion, the ethical concerns surrounding the potential interactions with technologically superior civilizations highlight the responsibilities and caution necessary as we pursue our cosmic aspirations represented by Dyson Spheres. By fostering dialogues built on mutual respect and empathy, we navigate the complexities of interstellar engagement, striving to create a future characterized by equitable relationships, environmental stewardship, and an enduring dedication to coexistence with all life forms we encounter in the boundless universe.

Finally, as we envision pathways toward technological balance within the context of Dyson Sphere enterprises, we open ourselves to reimagining how advanced civilizations might harmonize ambition and responsibility. The notion of achieving balance amidst the grandiosity of cosmic engineering compels us to reflect on our ethical obligations to each other, to our planet, and to potential life beyond it.

At the heart of this exploration lies the understanding that technological progress should not come at the expense of social equity, environmental sustainability, or cultural integrity. As future societies engage in the construction of Dyson Spheres and similar megastructures, they must do so with a conscious commitment to creating infrastructures that uphold the well-being of both current and future generations.

While the prospect of Dyson Spheres extends beyond Earthly boundaries, it also emphasizes the need to reassess our values and priorities. A focus on collective goals rooted in ethical considerations can guide the exploration of energy sources, enabling civilizations to navigate their ambitions while nurturing the planet's resources. The lessons learned from past environmental missteps on Earth must serve as a guiding principle in designing our cosmic engagement—encouraging sustainable practices that resonate through time and space.

Moreover, as we contemplate the implications of advanced technologies on societal structures, the pursuit of equality ought to be sovereign in any galactic endeavor. The ambitions associated with Dyson Sphere construction require collective action that reflects a diverse tapestry of experiences and perspectives. A cooperative spirit that fosters collaboration and equity amongst civilizations can forge pathways toward inclusive governance models, ensuring that decisions made in the cosmic realm resonate with shared values and explore the ideals of justice and fairness.

Through this lens, the quest for technological balance transforms into an invitation to reflect on our collective responsibilities toward one another, the environment, and the universe. As we step into a future where harnessing the energy of stellar constructs becomes a reality, we may do so with the awareness that our choices shape the trajectory of not just our civilizations but also of life across the cosmos.

It is the exploration of Dyson Spheres and their implications that ultimately illuminates the profound interconnectedness of life as we strive to grip the intricacies of existence. By working together and upholding principles of balance, we can create a shared cosmic narrative that embodies our highest aspirations, reflecting the enduring human spirit as we embrace our journey amidst the stars. Our ability to harmonize ambition and ethics will serve as a testament to what it means to be custodians of not just our destiny but also of existence itself as we traverse the vast and wondrous universe.

11.3. Advanced Propulsion Systems

The potential of advanced propulsion systems represents a critical pillar in realizing the ambitious endeavors of constructing Dyson Spheres, where the fundamental challenge extends beyond mere design to encompass the logistics of space travel and material mobilization. As humanity explores the feasibility of mega-engineering projects, understanding the nuances of propulsion technology becomes essential in navigating the complexities associated with transporting vast amounts of resources needed to build and maintain these cosmic structures.

At the forefront of propulsion technology is the necessity to overcome the limitations inherent in current chemical rockets, which are insufficient for the enormous demands of Dyson Sphere construction. This requires exploring advanced options that can provide greater thrust, efficiency, and range. One promising avenue is nuclear propulsion, where reactors yield continuous thrust over long durations, significantly enhancing travel capabilities within the solar system and potentially beyond. Nuclear thermal propulsion operates on the principle of heating a propellant carried in a reactor, offering much higher specific impulse compared to conventional fuels. This paradigm shift in propulsion technology would enable spacecraft to transport materials from celestial bodies, such as asteroids or moons, back to locations where Dyson Sphere components are assembled.

Another advanced propulsion technology that merits consideration is ion propulsion, which utilizes electric fields to accelerate ions and propel spacecraft. Ion engines have demonstrated high efficiency in long-duration missions, making them suitable for infrequent flights where speed is less critical. In a Dyson Sphere construction scenario, these engines could be employed in transporting satellites and equipment once material has been secured in orbit. Their efficiency ensures that vast distances can be traversed without heavy fuel costs, promising a sustainable logistical framework for the ongoing assembly tasks.

Additionally, concepts such as solar sails harnessing light pressure from the sun highlight the possibilities of propulsion devoid of conventional energy sources. By deploying reflective sails, spacecraft can ride the pressure of solar photons, gradually accelerating to reach substantial speeds over time. As a method of propulsion well-suited for deep-space exploration, depending on energy alternatives equates to aligning with the principles of sustainability central to Dyson Sphere logistics.

Interstellar travel introduces further dimensional complexities, and researchers must grapple with revolutionary concepts like theoretical warp drives or wormholes. These speculative technologies, while not yet realized, represent extraordinary potential for traversing distances that currently exceed conceivable time frames. The pursuit of advanced propulsion technologies drives the dialogue around humanity's aspirations for Dyson Sphere construction while concurrently urging innovations that may, one day, render notions of deep-space exploration practical.

Exploring these advanced propulsion systems also ties directly to the societal and ethical implications surrounding Dyson Sphere projects. As civilizations increasingly look beyond Earth, how society navigates its technological evolution becomes paramount. The advancements required for successful Dyson Sphere construction not only signify human ingenuity but also compel an ethical reflection on our responsibilities regarding energy use, environmental preservation, and the stewardship of resources.

In summary, the advancements in propulsion technologies form the backbone of any efforts related to Dyson Sphere construction. From nuclear thermal and ion propulsion systems to more speculative warp drive concepts, the capacity to mobilize materials across the vastness of space is essential to realize these grand ambitions. As we endeavor to harness stellar energies, our journey into the cosmos becomes intertwined with these propulsion capabilities, framing our narrative of exploration in the context of technological evolution and ethical responsibility. Through this lens, we position ourselves as responsible custodians of the energy and resources that tie our experiences to the infinite possibilities of the universe.

11.4. Quantum Mechanics and Macroengineering

In our exploration of quantum mechanics and macroengineering, we uncover the profound implications of integrating quantum principles into the design and operation of monumental structures like Dyson Spheres. Quantum mechanics, the foundation of modern physics, governs the behaviors of particles at atomic and subatomic levels, influencing everything from the properties of materials to the nature of energy transfer. As we venture into the theories surrounding Dyson Spheres, acknowledging the role of quantum mechanics not only unlocks new designs but also enriches our understanding of cosmic engineering.

To begin with, quantum mechanics can significantly influence the materials used in constructing a Dyson Sphere. The unique behaviors of particles at the quantum level allow for the development of advanced materials with extraordinary properties. For instance, researchers can explore metamaterials—substances engineered to have properties not usually found in nature, such as negative refractive indexes. Such materials could play a crucial role in optimizing energy absorption and minimizing energy losses within the energy-collecting units of a Dyson Sphere. By accounting for quantum effects during material synthesis, the efficiency of solar collectors can be dramatically enhanced, maximizing the energy captured from a star.

Moreover, the principles of superposition and entanglement bring exciting possibilities to information transmission within a Dyson Sphere. The dynamics of quantum entanglement could allow for instantaneous communication between different components of the Dyson Sphere infrastructure, enabling them to coordinate their operations seamlessly. This intricate web of interconnected devices may operate autonomously, continuously updating and optimizing energy collection strategies based on real-time data. The implications of this technology reach farther than mere electrical signals; they suggest a future where data transfer transcends traditional bandwidth limitations and creates a highly efficient network for monitoring and managing resources.

Furthermore, the implications of quantum mechanics extend into energy generation and conversion. Quantum tunneling, a phenomenon where particles can traverse energy barriers, could lead to advancements in energy storage systems, enhancing the capabilities of energy retention technologies essential for managing the abundant resources collected by a Dyson Sphere. By incorporating quantum principles into energy systems, we may create more efficient storage solutions that facilitate the seamless integration of harvested stellar energy into existing networks.

Additionally, the harmonization of quantum mechanics with macro-engineering may amplify our philosophical inquiries surrounding existence and the nature of life itself. As we navigate the complexities of designing a cosmos-spanning megastructure, we are invited to reconsider what it means to embrace fundamental principles of uncertainty and interconnectedness—hallmarks of quantum theory that echo throughout the universe. This renewed understanding reinforces the rich tapestry of life, technology, and cosmic exploration, as we come to realize that our pursuits are aligned with the profound nature of reality itself.

Finally, the confluence of quantum mechanics and macroengineering underscores the importance of technological ethics. In our ambition to construct Dyson Spheres, we must remain vigilant about the ethical considerations tied to advanced technologies. The power to manipulate materials and energy at quantum scales invites questions about our responsibilities as stewards of not just our planet but of the cosmic environments we engage with. As we intersect quantum principles with our grand aspirations, we stand at the precipice of an exciting and transformative journey—one that continues to illuminate pathways between the quantum world and the expansive universe awaiting our exploration.

In summary, the integration of quantum mechanics into the realm of macroengineering holds monumental potential for reshaping our understanding of Dyson Spheres and their implications on construction, sustainability, and societal evolution. By harnessing the principles of quantum physics, we can create structures capable of efficiently capturing the energy of stars, while simultaneously propelling our ethical discourse and philosophical reflections on existence amidst the fabric of the cosmos. As we explore the intricate dance between quantum mechanics and macroengineering, we reaffirm our roles as intelligent beings engaged in an ever-expanding journey—a journey that forever intertwines our aspirations with the profound laws that govern our universe.

11.5. Self-regulating Systems

The discussion of self-regulating systems in the context of Dyson Spheres reflects a profound integration of technology and ecology, highlighting the necessity for autonomous mechanisms that ensure resilience, efficiency, and sustainability in the operation of these monumental constructions. As humanity expands its ambitions toward harnessing the energy of stars, envisioning systems capable of self-management becomes essential. Such systems not only enhance operational efficacy but also embody the philosophical commitment to create technologies that are symbiotic with the ecosystems they inhabit.

At the core of self-regulating systems lies the concept of automation, which prioritizes adaptability and real-time decision-making. In the vast environment of a Dyson Sphere, a variety of parameters must be continuously monitored—ranging from energy output and structural integrity to environmental conditions influenced by solar activity. The integration of advanced sensors and feedback loops allows these systems to gather data, analyze it rapidly, and adjust operations accordingly. Imagine a network of autonomous drones and nano-sensors integrated throughout the Dyson Sphere, each tasked with monitoring specific components, energy collectors, and structural elements. Upon detecting anomalies, such as temperature fluctuations or signs of wear, these self-regulating units can automatically engage in repair protocols or redirect resources to optimize energy capture effectively.

Moreover, the adaptive capabilities of self-regulating systems extend beyond mere reaction to localized changes; they also enable strategic foresight. By employing predictive algorithms grounded in machine learning, these systems can anticipate fluctuations in stellar output, environmental impacts, and energetic demand across connected habitats. This capability enhances the resilience of the Dyson Sphere, as it can proactively adjust its operations to ensure consistent energy availability and mitigate potential disruptions. Should solar flares or gravitational fluctuations in the star system occur, self-regulating systems can dynamically adapt their operational parameters, ensuring stable energy delivery even under adverse conditions.

The role of such systems also underscores a commitment to ecological stewardship. Autonomous technologies can promote the sustainable use of resources by implementing energy-efficient practices that align with environmental principles. For instance, during periods of lower energy output from the star, self-regulating systems might prioritize power allocation for critical life-support functions, ensuring that habitats and installations maintain their essential operations while effectively managing energy consumption.

As we engage with the potential of self-regulating systems, the question of human involvement emerges prominently. While automation provides enhanced efficiency, these systems will require thoughtful oversight and governance. Systems designed to operate independently must also integrate ethical considerations that promote equitable access and responsible resource management. The governance structures that arise alongside these technologies will be crucial in ensuring that the benefits generated from the Dyson Sphere are distributed justly across connected societies, preventing the centralization of power that could lead to inequality or exploitation.

Moreover, the implications of self-regulating systems foster a deeper understanding of our relationship with technology. As civilizations harness the potential of Dyson Spheres through autonomous mechanisms, the role of humans as designers, stewards, and collaborators must be emphasized. This journey encourages a shift in perspective— one where technology is embraced as an extension of human agency, working in concert with life, rather than a replacement for it.

In summary, self-regulating systems represent a transformative aspect of Dyson Sphere operations, characterized by their ability to monitor, adapt, and enhance the functionality of these enormous constructs. The integration of automation, predictive capabilities, and ethical governance reflects humanity's pursuit of a sustainable future amongst the stars. As civilizations leverage these advanced technologies, the lessons learned in creating self-regulating systems will echo beyond individual societies, shaping the ethos of interstellar engagement while underscoring our commitment to harmony between technology and the cosmos. Through the lens of self-regulating systems, we can envision a future where Dyson Spheres not only symbolize immense power but also reflect the broader responsibilities we hold to ourselves and the universe at large.

12. Alien Societies and Technological Evolution

12.1. Indicators of Advanced Civilizations

Throughout human history, civilizations have gazed toward the stars, contemplating the presence and potential of life beyond our own planet. As we advance in our scientific understanding and technological capabilities, the search for extraterrestrial life increasingly leads us to consider the presence of advanced civilizations capable of extraordinary engineering feats, such as constructing Dyson Spheres. This subchapter delves into the indicators that may suggest the existence of these advanced societies and the implications of their technological prowess.

To begin with, the core premise of Dyson's original concept was that any civilization that had reached a significant technological level would find it imperative to harness the energy output of their star. The most flagrant indicator of such civilization would be the detection of an unusual amount of waste heat emanating from the vicinity of a star. Dyson theorized that as these civilizations absorbed energy, they would inevitably release heat as infrared radiation—the "waste" generated through the conversion of solar energy into usable power. Thus, one of the primary signs we might expect to uncover through astronomical observation is the signature of infrared emissions, observable through our advanced telescopes and astronomical sensors.

Additionally, advanced civilizations may exhibit changes in stellar luminosity indicative of energy-harvesting activity. A Dyson Sphere, or its variants, would create significant changes in the light patterns emitted by a star, possibly leading to periods of dimming or fluctuating intensity. For instance, the case of KIC 8462852—also known as Tabby's Star—sparked considerable discussion in the scientific community due to its irregular dimming patterns. While alternative explanations have emerged, such an anomaly compels researchers to consider the implications of potential extraterrestrial engineering. If further analysis of other stars yields similar results, we may pinpoint possible Dyson Sphere-like constructs across the galaxy.

Moreover, the search for advanced civilizations should also consider the context of significant engineering projects potentially visible from afar. Large-scale engineering activities, such as asteroid processing for Dyson Sphere construction or other megastructures, may produce observable disturbances in the solar system. Should a civilization actively mine materials from asteroids or planets to develop a Dyson Sphere, the resulting movement of celestial bodies through gravitational interactions or localized changes in their structure could become evident through careful monitoring of orbital dynamics.

The implications of discovering these indicators extend beyond mere curiosity; they pave the way for deeper inquiries into the complex narratives of advanced civilizations. The existence of extraterrestrial societies capable of harnessing stellar energy arguably raises questions about their societal organization, values, and governance. Would such engineers possess ecological sensibilities that align with sustainable practices, or might they engage in reckless exploitation reminiscent of past human behaviors?

Moreover, the detection of Dyson Sphere-like constructs or signatures would profoundly impact humanity's self-perception. As our species grapples with existential questions surrounding our cosmic solitude, discovering that we are not alone—especially potential creators of monumental engineering—would lead to an introspection about our trajectory as a civilization. The realization that other societies exist, thriving and innovating, invites us to reevaluate our aspirations, ethics, and responsibilities as we extend our reach into the cosmos.

In addition to understanding these indicators, we must consider the ethical implications of our interactions with advanced civilizations should they exist. How do we engage with societies capable of extraordinary technological achievements? The ethical frameworks guiding our approach must prioritize mutual respect, understanding, and cooperation while allowing for the coexistence of diverse perspectives and values. Cultural exchanges, if possible, should be rooted in reciprocity and an acknowledgment of the dignity of intelligent life.

In conclusion, the indicators of advanced civilizations capable of constructing Dyson Spheres hold immense significance for the ongoing quest to uncover the mysteries of the cosmos. From unusual infrared emissions to alterations in stellar luminosity and the movement of celestial bodies, these signs pave the way for deeper inquiries into the existence, values, and ethics of extraterrestrial societies. As we seek to understand the narratives woven into our shared cosmos, the exploration of potential advanced civilizations compels us to reflect on our responsibilities as stewards of knowledge, life, and technological evolution. The quest for answers remains an enduring testament to humanity's ambition to explore, connect, and harmonize with the universe that surrounds us.

As we engage further with the theoretical frameworks that explain how alien societies might structure their technologies to achieve Dyson-sphere-scale projects, we unravel exciting possibilities that challenge our understanding of engineering and civilization. The construction of such immense structures would not simply be a monumental achievement in itself; it would also necessitate the evolution of knowledge, innovation, and perhaps even the core values that define those advanced societies.

First, let us consider the types of technologies that might emerge in the pursuit of a Dyson Sphere. One potential manifestation is the integration of advanced AI systems capable of overseeing the construction and maintenance of these megastructures. For a civilization embarking on such monumental projects, AI could enhance predictive analytics, monitor energy capture efficiency, allocate resources effectively, and manage complex operations that would span vast distances across the solar system. Such intelligent systems would represent not only a technological leap but also a cultural shift towards collaboration between sentient beings and machines that transcend the typical boundaries of human labor.

Additionally, the concept of a modular Dyson Sphere—a design that incorporates smaller, autonomous units working together—could be particularly appealing among advanced civilizations. These modular constructs, known as Dyson Swarms, would be comprised of numerous individual satellites orbiting a star, allowing for flexible configurations and adjustments based on energy demands and environmental impact. The development of such structures would imply a society that values adaptability and sustainability, employing technologies that empower collaborative efforts while minimizing risks associated with a singular, rigid structure.

Furthermore, the deployment of advanced propulsion systems would play a crucial role in enabling efficient resource acquisition for Dyson Sphere construction. A civilization capable of engineering such megastructures would likely have developed highly efficient transportation technologies, such as advanced nuclear or ion propulsion systems, to facilitate the movement of materials harvested from asteroids or other celestial bodies. This innovation would open new avenues for interplanetary resource management and foster an economy built on cooperation and trade across the cosmos.

As we explore technological frameworks integral to alien societies, we must also consider the ethical principles that may arise from their interactions with burgeoning powers in space. Collaboration and shared knowledge could become core values fueling progress in cosmic engineering endeavors; however, advanced civilizations must navigate the delicate balance between growth and monopoly on resources. Promoting equitable approaches toward resource management could ultimately define how they shape galactic economies and foster cooperation among species.

In both the construction and operation of Dyson Spheres, the advanced civilizations embracing such technologies would grapple with their impact on life within their ecosystems. Will they prioritize ecological sustainability, ensuring that their activities do not impinge on the natural habitats of other species? This interplay between technological prowess and ecological stewardship sets the frame for future discussions surrounding not just the responsibility of owning such technologies but also their inherent obligation to protect diverse life forms.

In summary, the theoretical frameworks surrounding alien technologies capable of achieving Dyson-sphere-scale projects challenge our understanding of civilization and engineering. As we contemplate the implications of such structures, we acknowledge the significance of advanced AI, collaborative designs, and efficient propulsion systems in shaping the values and responsibilities of those who create them. By studying these technologies, we may glean not only insights into the potential achievements of extraterrestrial societies but also valuable lessons that can guide our collective journey toward a sustainable and interconnected future in the cosmos.

As we turn our focus to the remarkable potential of cultural exchange across light years, the prospect of engaging with advanced civilizations beckons as both an exhilarating opportunity and an intricate challenge. The intersection of cosmos-spanning constructs like Dyson Spheres invites us to envision a future characterized by collaboration, dialogue, and shared knowledge—a narrative that resonates deeply with humanity's intrinsic desire to connect with and learn from others across the universe.

In the realm of cosmic engagement, the idea of cultural exchange conjures visions of mutual understanding and cooperation between civilizations capable of remarkable feats. If humanity were to encounter advanced societies proficient in building Dyson Spheres, the scope of these engagements would extend beyond mere technological exchanges. The rich tapestry of shared experiences, philosophies, and artistic vibrancies could pave the way for transformative dialogues that transcend the limitations of language and geography.

However, navigating these encounters requires careful consideration of the complexities and nuances that characterize interactions on an astronomical scale. The ethical dimensions surrounding cross-civilizational exchanges must remain paramount. Humility and respect will be essential guiding principles as humanity engages with potentially disparate cultures, each shaped by its unique narratives, environments, and values. For establishing meaningful connections, we may need to consider strategies that foster open dialogues and prioritize the recognition of cultural diversity as strengths rather than barriers.

Moreover, the potential for advanced civilizations to possess vastly different technologies and ideologies raises critical questions about power dynamics. Engaging with civilizations far superior to our own could lead to imbalances in influence, prompting us to confront uncomfortable reflections about agency and autonomy. With an awareness of historical legacies surrounding colonization, exploitation, and cultural erasure, we should strive to uphold values that promote equal partnership and enhance the dignity of all parties involved in cosmic interactions.

In considering the mechanics of cultural exchange, the universality of music, mathematics, and sound emerges as critical connecting threads. Just as cosmic phenomena resonate through the harmonies of existence, the artistic expressions forged by civilizations can serve as powerful vehicles for silent storytelling. Through communal appreciation of each other's crafts, art forms, and philosophies, societies can construct connective bridges that lay the groundwork for enduring relationships.

Notably, the integration of shared technologies can foster collaborative innovation. As civilizations confront energy challenges and explore the capabilities of Dyson Spheres, sharing logics, designs, and scientific principles may pave the way for collective advancements that transcend societal barriers. These collaborations can invigorate scientific inquiry, as each civilization brings its unique perspectives and experiences to the table, enriching the reciprocal exchange of knowledge.

In summary, the vision of cultural exchange across light years invites profound reflections on the aspirations, responsibilities, and ethical frameworks governing interstellar engagements. As humanity yearns to connect with intelligent life capable of constructing Dyson Spheres, we must endeavor to navigate these encounters with humility and a commitment to equity and respect. By integrating art, science, and shared experiences into the tapestry of our cosmic journeys, we can build a future defined by collaboration and understanding—reflecting our shared potential to thrive amid the vastness of the universe.

In examining the ethical considerations that arise from interstellar contexts, we confront essential questions regarding our responsibilities toward other intelligent civilizations. The exploration of advanced civilizations capable of constructing Dyson Spheres compels us to reflect on our engagement with these societies, emphasizing the need for ethical frameworks that ensure respectful and equitable interactions across cosmic distances.

When contemplating the discovery and interaction with extraterrestrial societies that have achieved monumental technological feats, the specter of power dynamics looms large. Often, superior technological capabilities may inadvertently translate into potential domination or coercion. As we encounter civilizations that could manipulate stellar energy and resources, humanity must thoughtfully grapple with the ethical implications of such power disparities.

At the forefront of these ethical considerations lies the notion of coexistence. How do we engage with other intelligent species in a manner that honors their agency and value systems? The long-established principles of mutual respect and equity become imperative as we navigate the complexities of interstellar relationships. Establishing a foundation of understanding can help mitigate misunderstandings and foster a sense of partnership rather than competition, helping to shape a narrative centered on collaborative progress.

Moreover, engaging ethically with advanced civilizations also compels us to address the potential ecological implications of interstellar interactions. The act of energy harvesting—especially from a Dyson

Sphere—could have unintended consequences on nearby ecosystems or planets. Protecting such environments must remain a priority in our ethical framework, ensuring that our technological pursuits do not compromise the intrinsic value of other life forms.

In addition, the prospect of encountering advanced civilizations raises important questions about knowledge sharing. While vibrant exchanges of information and insights could enrich both parties, we must consider the power dynamics and motivations that inform these interactions. How can we ensure that the benefits from such exchanges extend equitably among different cultures? The principles guiding negotiations must prioritize not only collective gain but also the dignity and right of all life forms to coexist responsibly.

Furthermore, the ethical discourse surrounding interstellar interactions invites reflections on our own cultural underpinnings. As we embrace the quest for Dyson Spheres and other cosmic endeavors, a deep awareness of our histories becomes vital. The ethical frameworks we erect must explicitly acknowledge past mistakes surrounding colonialism and exploitation while ensuring that our aspirations for progress are framed by a commitment to justice, compassion, and cultural sensitivity.

In summary, the exploration of ethical concerns inherent in interstellar contexts offers a vital narrative for engaging with advanced civilizations. As humanity contemplates contact with other intelligent beings capable of building Dyson Spheres, we must prioritize principles of coexistence, ecological responsibility, knowledge equity, and cultural respect. Through this ethical lens, we can foster relationships rooted in mutual understanding and shared aspirations—crafting a cosmic narrative that honors the dignity of all life while harmonizing our quests among the stars.

As we imagine the road toward achieving technological balance in the context of Dyson Sphere construction, we find ourselves amidst a profound opportunity to define our role as stewards of energy, innovation, and ethical responsibility. The ambition to harness stellar energy through such colossal projects is coupled with the necessity to ensure that our advancements serve the greater good, promoting equitable access, sustainable practices, and environmental preservation.

At its core, the pursuit of technological balance emphasizes a reimagining of our relationship with technology itself. It compels us to address the question: How can we harness the extraordinary potential offered by Dyson Spheres while remaining committed to ethical stewardship? Striving for balance within our technological pursuits means acknowledging the intricate intertwining of progress with responsibility—where the benefits generated by energy harvesting are distributed equitably among diverse communities.

One of the defining characteristics of achieving balance in Dyson Sphere technologies lies in recognizing ecological limits. The energy captured from stars must be utilized in harmony with surrounding ecosystems, ensuring that resource management does not jeopardize the delicate intricacies of life on other planets. As we delve into the possibilities of interstellar interactions, the prioritization of sustainable practices must remain paramount. We should actively explore ways to implement ecological principles in the decision-making processes surrounding energy use and resource extraction, inviting ethical reflections on our responsibilities as cosmic stewards.

Moreover, the implications of technological balance guide our understanding of social structures that may arise in the wake of Dyson Sphere construction. The commitment to equity and justice becomes essential in permitting all planetary inhabitants to benefit from advanced energy sources and technologies. Balancing power dynamics necessitates frameworks that uphold fairness, transparency, and inclusivity—ensuring that communities have a voice in resource management and decision-making systems. By prioritizing collaboration rather than hierarchy, societies can embrace a spirit of cooperation that fosters peace and collective advancement.

As we engage the idea of technological balance, it is essential to foster dialogues among the various stakeholders involved in Dyson Sphere construction and operation, ensuring their ethical implications are thoroughly examined. This proactive engagement, driven by interdisciplinary collaboration across scientific, cultural, and social dimensions, allows us to weave together diverse perspectives and values into a holistic framework that aspires to create meaningful and sustainable futures.

In summary, the journey toward achieving technological balance in the context of Dyson Sphere construction opens up significant avenues for navigating the intersection of ambition and responsibility. As we strive to harness the energy of stars, the principles of equity, ecological stewardship, and cooperative governance must serve as guiding stars—illuminating our aspirations while reminding us of our fundamental duty to each other, our planet, and the universe. Through technological balance, we embrace not only the promise of progress but also the opportunity to cultivate a legacy that celebrates the interconnectedness of all life across the cosmos.

12.2. Theoretical Frameworks for Alien Technologies

Throughout the ages, humankind has gazed up at the stars with wonder, asking questions both profound and whimsical. We have mapped their movements, told stories about their origins, and even ventured a few gentle steps towards their bright complexity. But what if our loftiest ambitions were no longer tethered by the familiar confines of our planet and technology? What if our imagination scaffolded a bridge to living among the stars themselves?

The theoretical Dyson Sphere, a colossal structure capable of capturing the entirety of a star's energy output, ignites such dreams. While largely speculative, the mere notion of such an existence allows us to explore the boundaries of our potential, both scientifically and philosophically. In "Living with a Dyson Sphere," we embark on a detailed exploration of these hypothetical alien megastructures, their implications, and the possibilities they possess within the vast theater of the universe. Join me, Eileen Patricia Miller, as we unravel the strands of science, technology, and imagination to envision a life where the cosmos is no longer a distant spectator but an integral part of human existence.

Theoretical frameworks for alien technologies concerning Dyson Spheres invite us to contemplate the vast array of scientific advancements that advanced civilizations might achieve. From the macro to the nano scales, we will explore how different areas of technology could converge to enable the construction and operation of such colossal energy-harvesting structures.

Harnessing stellar energy, for instance, would likely require a profound understanding of both astrophysics and materials science. It's conceivable that an advanced civilization would develop novel materials capable of withstanding the extreme conditions surrounding a star. The use of metamaterials could open new pathways to efficiently capture, transform, and transmit energy, ultimately leading to the creation of a self-sustaining infrastructure. These technically sophisticated structures might employ principles of quantum physics to optimize energy absorption, and perhaps utilize nanotech to form self-repairing components, efficiently maintaining structural integrity and functionality.

Similarly, propulsion technologies would evolve to support interstellar logistics. Continued advancements could include nuclear propulsion systems, ion drives, or even theoretical concepts like warp drives, enhancing the capability to transport materials across astronomical distances. This presents a compelling image of civilization-scale logistics, where resources ranging from asteroids to comets become integral to sustaining an economy based on stellar energy harvesting.

Examining communication technologies is also essential when considering the theoretical frameworks for alien technologies. Advanced civilizations may develop methods of transmitting information that could transcend the traditional barriers of electromagnetic waves, possibly utilizing quantum entanglement to allow instantaneous communication across galaxies. Such innovations would revolutionize how societies interact, fostering an interconnected cosmic community that transcends light-year distances.

Moreover, the governance of such advanced technologies raises questions about the frameworks that alien societies might adopt. Would their organizational structures reflect hierarchical dominance, or would they embody egalitarian principles emphasizing collaboration? The commitment to sustainability and ethical stewardship could be foundational to their survival and success, creating systems that prioritize the collective good over individual interests.

Scientific exploration is woven deeply into the fabric of these cosmic narratives, revealing how advancements in technology resonate with cultural evolution. With each leap toward harnessing stellar energy, a civilization may simultaneously evolve its philosophical and ethical perspectives, learning from the profound responsibilities that come with wielding such power. This reflection raises questions: how would the societal values shift as a civilization embraces its potential to manipulate cosmic forces? Would greater access to energy lead to an era of peace and cooperation, or could it exacerbate inequalities?

In conclusion, the theoretical frameworks for alien technologies related to Dyson Spheres compel us to engage more deeply with expansive narratives that celebrate ingenuity, cooperation, and responsibility. As we envision the remarkable capacities of civilizations capable of reaching these cosmic heights, we are invited to reflect not only on the possibilities but also on the ethical imperatives that must guide our designs, aspirations, and relationships as we reach for the stars. Ultimately, the pursuit of harnessing stellar energies transforms our understandings and experiences as we navigate the challenges and wonders of existence amidst the universe's vast canvas.

12.3. Cultural Exchange Across Light Years

Cultural Exchange Across Light Years is a rich tapestry woven from the threads of imagination, ambition, and the potential intersection of diverse civilizations. As humanity embarks on its journey toward constructing megastructures like Dyson Spheres, the prospect of engaging with extraterrestrial societies introduces both thrilling opportunities and complex challenges. This exploration invites an examination of how cultures might connect, share knowledge, and collaboratively navigate the vastness of the cosmos, creating vibrant exchange systems that transcend planetary boundaries.

The framework for cultural exchange across light years must first acknowledge the varying degrees of advancement among civilizations. The unequal development of technologies and social structures could create significant barriers to understanding and collaboration. Advanced societies capable of constructing Dyson Spheres may possess not only the engineering acumen but also unique ethical perspectives shaped by their histories, philosophies, and environmental contexts. As we consider potential encounters with such civilizations, we must embrace a mindset of humility, open-mindedness, and curiosity—acknowledging that our values and approaches may not align perfectly with theirs.

Central to productive cultural exchanges is the importance of communication. The universality of concepts such as mathematics, sound, and art could serve as bridging mechanisms, transcending linguistic barriers and fostering connections. Music, for instance, resonates deeply with the human experience; it may well emerge as a powerful medium for expression and understanding, enabling dialogues that incorporate emotional and philosophical dimensions. Compositions inspired by cosmic phenomena or sharing experiences of existence among the stars could inspire collaborative artistic endeavors, fueling a sense of community that unites disparate civilizations under a shared affinity for creativity.

Moreover, engaging with advanced civilizations opens avenues for collaborative exploration in fields such as science and technology. The opportunity to share knowledge about energy systems, ecological management, and resource utilization can foster a symbiotic relationship that benefits all parties involved. This exchange of information can catalyze advancements that align with sustainable practices, spurring us to reconsider our approaches to resource management, innovation, and ethical engagement.

However, the implications of cultural exchange extend beyond tangible benefits; they compel us to confront the ethical dimensions of such interactions. The potential for unequal power dynamics is significant when engaging with a civilization possessing advanced technologies. We must establish ethical frameworks that prioritize mutual respect and equity, ensuring that interactions promote understanding rather than exploitation. The lessons derived from human history can illuminate the path forward, guiding us to foster relationships based on empathy, appreciation, and shared aspirations.

The exploration of cultural exchange across light years also invites us to re-evaluate the narrative of humanity's place in the universe. Dis encounters with diverse civilizations could prompt profound reflections on identity, purpose, and belonging. In recognizing that we are part of a broader cosmic community, we may embrace a more inclusive definition of humanity that transcends terrestrial confines and acknowledges the interconnectedness of all sentient beings.

As we envision the future, the potential for cultural exchanges across light years unlocks new narratives that celebrate collaboration, creativity, and shared wisdom. Exploring the cosmos becomes a collective endeavor, where diverse civilizations engage in symbiotic dialogues that enrich both their experiences while furthering cosmic exploration. In this journey, we can cultivate a culture that values compassion, equity, and cooperation—one that reflects our innate longing to connect with the universe and its myriad of life forms.

Through this lens, cultural exchange across light years embodies a transformative journey that transcends the boundaries of space and time. By navigating the complexities of interstellar interactions with respect and curiosity, we can foster a future where the collective ambitions of diverse civilizations become intertwined in the narratives of existence. As we step into the cosmic realm, we embrace not only the possibilities that await us but also our responsibility to seek harmonious coexistence with all life that shares the stars.

12.4. Ethical Concerns in Interstellar Contexts

As we contemplate the implications of interstellar expansions fueled by advanced technologies like Dyson Spheres, ethical concerns inevitably emerge. The very idea of engaging with extraterrestrial civilizations capable of monumental engineering feats invites reflections on our responsibilities as stewards of life, knowledge, and innovation. This examination encompasses a wide array of ethical dilemmas related to cultural exchanges, societal interactions, and the preservation of our own identities in the face of the unknown.

An initial layer of ethical considerations arises from the power dynamics inherent in cross-cultural engagements. If humanity were to encounter a civilization that has successfully constructed a Dyson Sphere, it can naturally shift the balance of power. The advanced technological capabilities of such a society might create a scenario where an unequal power dynamic emerges—a civilization possessing advanced energy harnessing technologies could dominate or exploit those less developed. Therefore, establishing ethical frameworks that prioritize respect, cooperation, and equitable partnerships is necessary to avoid historical patterns of conquest and oppression.

The implications of potential cultural misunderstanding also warrant careful consideration. Approaching an advanced civilization with our values, social norms, and expectations may not always resonate. There lies the risk of imposing our perspectives on others, neglecting the rich tapestries of their histories. Sensitivity and open-mindedness will be key when navigating the complexities of interstellar interactions, ensuring that we remain receptive to diverse worldviews and cultural expressions that may differ markedly from our own.

Moreover, ethical concerns extend to the environmental responsibilities that accompany interstellar interactions. The vast scope of energy harnessing through Dyson Spheres invites questions about the ecological footprints of advanced civilizations. As we engage with extraterrestrial societies, we must remain committed to safeguarding the integrity of their planetary systems and ecosystems. The quest for energy must not disregard the delicate balances that sustain life, and awareness of ecological stewardship must guide our actions among the stars.

Equally pressing is the consideration of knowledge sharing, particularly if we encounter civilizations that have developed technologies far beyond our own. The ethical questions surrounding knowledge transfer become vital—how can we ensure that information exchanged is used to uplift rather than exploit? What protections should be in place to safeguard cultural identities and prevent the erosion of unique societal values? Fostering dialogue built on mutual respect can nurture relationships that transcend mere transactions, enriching our understanding of life in diverse forms.

The ethical implications surrounding encounters with alien civilizations also invite reflection on our own values, practices, and developmental trajectories. As we explore Dyson Sphere technologies and contemplate their far-reaching potentials, the lessons we glean from the engagement should resonate deeply within our societies. The pursuit of technological ambition must be grounded in a commitment to ethical considerations that prioritize the well-being of all life forms, including ourselves.

Finally, as we envision a future marked by interstellar engagement, it becomes crucial to establish frameworks for ethical governance. These frameworks should empower individuals and communities to protect their rights, ensuring collective decision-making processes that uphold fairness and equity. Encouraging interdisciplinary dialogues that transcend scientific specialties can further enhance our capacity to address the nuanced ethical considerations inherent in interstellar interactions.

In conclusion, the ethical concerns associated with interstellar contexts present intricate challenges and opportunities as we grapple with our place in the cosmos. The quest for Dyson Sphere technologies compels us to confront historical legacies, embrace cultural understanding, and cultivate a sense of responsibility towards all life. As we envision a future of cosmic engagements, it is incumbent upon us to forge pathways marked by equity, respect, and integrity—ensuring that our narratives are enriched by the collaborative spirit that defines humanity's journey through the stars. As we strive for interconnected futures, our ethical frameworks will be essential in shaping the legacy we leave for all civilizations navigating the expansive universe together.

In the context of potential interstellar interactions, envisioning pathways toward technological balance holds profound significance. The concept of technological balance becomes a pivotal idiom through which societies can harmonize their ambitions with ethical responsibilities and cultural identities while exploring Dyson Sphere technologies and other advanced engineering pursuits.

At its core, technological balance necessitates a conscious approach to innovation, ensuring that progress reflects communal values rather than merely driving individual success. This principle becomes especially crucial as advanced civilizations contemplate the pursuit of megastructures capable of harnessing stellar energy. The implementation of Dyson Sphere technologies must foster adaptation to resource availability and social equity—an imperative that underscores the responsibilities assumed by the civilizations engaged in such cosmic engineering.

Central to achieving balance is the recognition of the finite nature of resources, even among the vastness of space. As civilizations harness energy from stars, it becomes necessary to prioritize sustainable practices that do not overextend their capabilities or devastate ecosystems. This sustainable model compels societies to create frameworks that promote resourcefulness, ecological respect, and attentiveness to the interconnected networks of life, aligning technological advancements with the teachings of stewardship echoed in cultures across the world.

Moreover, fostering collaborative governance structures emerges as a fundamental strategy in the pursuit of technological balance. The societal frameworks tasked with overseeing Dyson Sphere operations must prioritize inclusive decision-making. Encouraging participation and representation from diverse communities ensures that the voices of all stakeholders shape the discourse surrounding the equitable use of resources and the distribution of energy harvested from celestial bodies. In developing governance frameworks grounded in shared responsibility and ethical reflection, advanced civilizations can cultivate societies that embrace the ideals of cooperation and sustainability.

As societies evolve alongside their technologies, the impact of technological balance extends beyond operational efficiency—inviting a re-evaluation of cultural identities and values. Engaging with the implications of Dyson Sphere constructions invites societies to reflect critically on their ambitions. The aspirations tied to harnessing stellar energy can serve as a catalyst for emerging narratives that spotlight sustainable development and ethical consciousness, ultimately fostering unity within the diverse tapestry of cultures across the cosmos.

In turn, the interplay between technology and culture invites us to examine how our technological advancement shapes philosophical and ethical inquiries. Engaging with the principles driving technological progression can prompt societies to reflect on their responsibilities, interconnectedness, and commitments to justice and equity. The pursuit of a Dyson Sphere becomes not only an endeavor marked by impressive engineering but also an opportunity for refining our values—encouraging us to strive toward a future where technological achievements resonate harmoniously within the broader ecological context.

In summary, navigating pathways toward achieving technological balance amidst the ambition to construct Dyson Spheres invites profound considerations regarding sustainability, resource management, and cultural identity. As civilizations engage in their quests for cosmic energy, they must do so with a commitment to collective well-being, fostering governance frameworks that embrace inclusion and ethical reflection. By harmonizing our ambitions with responsibilities, we can shape a future defined not just by progress, but also by accountability and integrity—creating a legacy that strengthens our collective identity within the boundless cosmos.

As we embark on the exploration of the theoretical frameworks surrounding advanced civilizations, we find ourselves drawn to the potential for groundbreaking discoveries that could fundamentally reshape our understanding of life, technology, and existence itself. The pursuit of Dyson Spheres signifies not just a monumental engineering effort but also embodies humanity's quest for knowledge —a quest that invites us to imagine what transformative discoveries might arise from our endeavors.

One of the most immediate avenues for potential discoveries lies in the astrobiological implications surrounding Dyson Spheres. If we were to uncover a Dyson Sphere or its remnants, it would signal the existence of sophisticated societies capable of harnessing stellar energy. The realization that intelligent life engages with the universe in such grand ways would prompt humanity to reevaluate its place among the stars, ushering in an era of exploration marked by curiosity and wonder.

Moreover, should we encounter alien civilizations achieving remarkable engineering feats, the intercultural exchanges that ensue could yield transformative insights that influence our philosophical, ethical, and technological discourses. Knowledge transfer may propel developments in areas such as sustainable practices, energy management, and resource allocation—creating pathways toward a future characterized by cooperation and shared advancement. The vibrancy of these exchanges may inspire growth across various fields, from science and technology to arts and culture.

In addition, the encounter with advanced civilizations may lead to new methods of communication and collaboration, dramatically altering our approaches to dialogue. The evidence of gigastructures like Dyson Spheres may converge interpretations of shared existence and collectivism, reframing how humanity engages in interpersonal relations. The insights gained from cultural exchanges could yield narratives that transcend planetary boundaries, fostering a sense of communal belonging within a broader cosmic context.

The implications of potentially discovering ecological practices employed by advanced extraterrestrial civilizations also hold immense significance for humanity. The understanding of sustainability on a galactic scale could invite reflections on the responsibilities tied to technological prowess. The teachings from civilizations achieving Dyson Sphere success may empower us to reevaluate our environmental practices, incorporating holistic approaches that honor and protect the intricate ecosystems we inhabit.

However, while we contemplate these transformative discoveries, we must also navigate the challenges they may invoke within our societies. The implications of uncovering Dyson Spheres and engaging with advanced civilizations may evoke existential questions surrounding power dynamics, ethical considerations, and social cohesion. The narrative choices we make in response to such discoveries will be fundamental to shaping our emerging identity as interstellar citizens.

In summary, the potential discoveries that could arise from the pursuit of Dyson Sphere technologies encompass profound implications for humanity's growth, understanding, and responsibility toward our place in the cosmos. As we continue this journey of exploration, we must not only engage in the wonders that beckon but also embrace the ethical considerations that arise. By advocating for cooperation, sustainability, and shared advancement, we position ourselves to forge a meaningful legacy—one that gratefully returned reaches toward the stars while celebrating the diversity and resilience of life across the universe.

As we embark on the imaginative journey of envisioning a future civilization shaped by the realizations of Dyson Sphere technologies, we are prompted to reflect on the transformative impact these constructs may have on society, culture, and human aspirations. The quest for harnessing stellar energy encapsulates the essence of our inherent desire to explore, innovate, and strive for greatness, turning the act of reaching for the stars into a powerful narrative of progress and interconnectedness.

One of the most profound implications of Dyson Sphere technologies lies in the potential for societal evolution. As energy abundance becomes a reality, the socio-economic structures that define our civilizations may undergo significant transformations. The very foundation of resource allocation shifts from scarcity-driven competition to collaboration and mindful management of abundance—setting the stage for a paradigm shift in how we approach governance, economics, and quality of life.

In this new societal context, principles of cooperative governance may emerge, emphasizing the importance of inclusion, equity, and sustainability in decision-making processes. A future civilization inspired by Dyson Sphere realizations may adopt collaborative frameworks that ensure collective participation in resource management, fostering a culture of shared responsibility and stewardship. By actively engaging communities in shaping the trajectory of energy use, societies can cultivate a deeper sense of ownership and accountability.

Moreover, the cultural landscape of future civilizations may reflect the harmonious blend of science and art, as the pursuit of Dyson Sphere technologies reshapes our narratives and expressions. The interconnectedness of life, energy, and creativity can inspire an artistic renaissance, where diverse forms of expression celebrate the possibilities of harnessing stellar power. Musical compositions, visual arts, and literature may emerge as conduits for exploring the relationship between human experience and the cosmos, invoking collective reflections that transcend planetary boundaries.

The educational frameworks within these future societies would likely adapt to reflect the values and knowledge born from Dyson Sphere technologies. An emphasis on interdisciplinary learning—

merging science, ethics, and the arts—would empower individuals to become informed stewards of energy and resources. Teaching future generations about the intricacies of cosmic engineering while embedding ethical responsibilities within educational curricula can cultivate a mindset that embraces innovation while prioritizing sustainability and respect for all forms of life.

Furthermore, in the pursuit of constructing Dyson Spheres and engaging with advanced civilizations, ethical considerations must endure at the forefront of societal evolution. As interstellar citizens, we must navigate questions of power dynamics, resource management, and the potential ecological impact of our actions. The narratives that unfold within these future societies must reflect a commitment to kindness, equity, and collaboration—ensuring that our aspirations for progress do not inadvertently favor a select few at the expense of others.

In conclusion, imagining a future civilization influenced by Dyson Sphere technologies compels us to consider the profound societal, cultural, and ethical implications of harnessing stellar energy. The quest encourages us to advocate for cooperative governance, foster artistic expression, and cultivate holistic educational frameworks that embrace the interconnectedness of all life. As we step into this cosmic future, let us strive to ensure that our narrative reflects the best of our humanity—a legacy marked by progress, compassion, and mutual respect among all inhabitants of the universe.

As we contemplate the effects of constructing Dyson Spheres on the solar system, we invite reflections on the transformative implications such monumental engineering feats might evoke. The potential for these megastructures to harness stellar energy not only heralds a new era of resource management but also introduces complex dynamics that could reshape the relationship between humanity, technology, and the celestial environments surrounding us.

The immediate impact of a Dyson Sphere on our solar system entails several physical and ecological considerations. The alteration of energy distribution resulting from energy harvesting must be addressed, as the dynamics of solar radiation received by planets may shift dramatically. Once stars' energy absorption becomes significant, the climates, weather patterns, and ecological balances of neighboring celestial bodies could undergo significant changes. Such shifts may have cascading effects on the evolution and sustainability of life on these worlds, urging us to consider the long-term consequences of our engineering ambitions.

Moreover, the gravitational interactions within the solar system will require scrutiny as a Dyson Sphere is constructed and employed. These structures will exert immense gravitational forces on their surroundings—potentially complicating orbital dynamics for planets, moons, and smaller celestial bodies alike. The influx of new masses alters gravitational balances and could lead to shifts in orbits or establish new trajectories, introducing uncertainties in the stability of celestial arrangements. Factors extending to the Hawking radiation from dying stars or perturbations caused by dwarf planets will surely require meticulous monitoring and adjustment mechanisms.

From a technological perspective, constructing Dyson Spheres motivates unprecedented advancements in materials science, robotics, and nanotechnology—and these developments ripple through societies on Earth and beyond. The skills acquired and innovations reached in executing such monumental projects will invariably inspire other industrious pursuits, fostering a culture of exploration and technophilia that echoes through the solar system. Planning megastructures will encourage societies to adopt principles of sustainability, resourcefulness, and ecological awareness, creating a future marked by responsible growth.

However, as we ascend toward such cosmic ambitions, we must also critically evaluate the societal dynamics emerging from these endeavors. The energy captured through a Dyson Sphere could enhance humanity's collective experience by abolishing energy scarcity, fundamentally transforming how communities interact with resources. Societies may pivot toward collaboration over competition, integrating shared objectives to optimize energy use and seek sustainable practices across the cosmos.

Yet, the implications of Dyson Sphere technology transcend mere technological achievements; they raise complex ethical considerations encompassing stewardship, environmental integrity, and intercultural interaction. As humanity expands into the cosmos, we must wrestle with the responsibilities of managing resources to prevent negative ecological impacts on neighboring celestial environments. Living in harmony with the dynamics of the solar system will extend beyond technological prowess down to ethical frameworks.

In summary, the impacts of Dyson Sphere construction on the solar system could elicit transformative changes across environmental, technological, and societal dimensions. As we navigate these emerging trajectories, we must remain committed to ensuring that our cosmic ambitions are guided by principles of sustainability, mutual respect, and ecological responsibility. As we position ourselves as stewards of energy and life, the quest for Dyson Spheres invites us to engage thoughtfully with the complexities of existence among the stars and to honor our shared destiny within the cosmic tapestry.

Imagining alternative futures for megaengineering ventures like the Dyson Sphere compels us to venture beyond the boundaries of our current understandings of technological capabilities. As humanity endeavors to harness the stars, the possibilities unfold in myriad directions, opening a narrative that challenges us to envision how our societal and ecological realities might transform across a cosmic landscape defined by innovation and interdependence.

One potential future may emerge from the realization of a Dyson Sphere's construction and the resulting energy abundance—ushering in an era where resource constraints cease to stifle creativity and exploration. In this paradigm, the commitment to sustainability and ethical resource management could catalyze advancements in various fields, from renewable technologies and ecological engineering to artistic expressions that celebrate the interconnectedness of life.

The cultural renaissance propelled by Dyson Sphere energies might redefine humanity's role in the universe—transforming us from mere inhabitants of a planet to active participants and caretakers of cosmic ecosystems.

Alternatively, we may envision a scenario steeped in caution—a future where humanity's reckless pursuit of cosmic energies leads to ecological degradation or conflicts among advanced societies. The opportunity for exploitation may emerge among civilizations vying for control over resources associated with Dyson Sphere constructions. This speculative trajectory serves as a warning, urging us to recognize the complexities tied to technological development and the impacts these undertakings exert on interstellar relationships and ecosystems.

The underlying narratives of alternative futures may also encompass the exploration of new forms of governance and ethical practices within interstellar contexts. As civilizations engage in megaengineering projects, questions of equitable resource distribution and cultural preservation become paramount. Different models of governance may emerge based on collaboration, transparency, and shared decision-making—shaping societies that prioritize collective well-being and ecological stewardship over competition.

Further, alternative futures may highlight the importance of technological harmony and balance among civilizations— establishing principles that govern responsible resource management and exploration of adjacent celestial bodies. As societies aspire to achieve Dyson Sphere technologies, they may encounter complex challenges related to environmental preservation, risk management, and ethical interconnections with potential cultures throughout the cosmos. The lessons learned from navigating these dilemmas may inform future discourse on balancing progress with moral integrity, ensuring that the pursuit of technological advancement reflects a commitment to cooperation.

In summary, imagining alternative futures for megaengineering ventures like Dyson Spheres invites us to explore various pathways of innovation, collaboration, and ethical reflection. The narratives that unfold reveal the complexities of our aspirations amidst the stars, urging us to consider the consequences of our actions and the responsibilities we embrace. As we journey forward, the exploration of alternative futures serves as a catalyst for dialogue that enhances our understanding of the interconnectedness of life and technological development, paving the way for sustainable coexistence in the expansive cosmic realms we endeavor to understand.

12.5. Quests for Technological Balance

In the ongoing pursuit of understanding the implications of hypothetical structures like Dyson Spheres, we must engage in a quest for technological balance that harmonizes ambition with ethical responsibility and ecological stewardship. The prospect of constructing such colossal structures to harness stellar energy signifies both an incredible opportunity and a formidable challenge for advanced civilizations. Balancing technological advancement with the need to respect natural laws and cultural identities becomes imperative as we consider the future trajectory of civilizations capable of such endeavours.

To achieve this balance, civilizations must prioritize sustainable practices and community engagement in the operational and construction phases of Dyson Sphere projects. The integration of ecological considerations into these ambitious engineering feats will ensure that energy harvesting does not compromise the integrity of ecosystems surrounding the structures. For instance, the deployment of advanced materials and robotic systems must focus not only on efficiency but also on minimizing ecological footprints—encouraging responsible resource management that respects the delicate balances present in the solar system.

Moreover, maintaining a commitment to social equity across advanced civilizations becomes essential in fostering stability and inclusivity. As societies harness the immense power derived from Dyson Spheres, they must actively engage all sectors of their populations in decision-making processes regarding energy allocation and resource management. Establishing governance frameworks prioritizing fairness, transparency, and collaboration can nurture a culture of togetherness while preventing inequalities from arising in energy access.

A crucial component of technological balance lies in fostering collaboration among diverse civilizations, emphasizing shared hopes and collective aspirations. As contact is made with extraterrestrial societies, the dialogue surrounding cosmic energy management must flow freely and openly, promoting cooperative frameworks that deepen understanding and create lasting partnerships. By prioritizing collective goals of stewardship alongside energy harvesting, we create an opportunity for rich exchanges of knowledge, art, and philosophy that enrich the human experience while celebrating diverse life forms.

As we anticipate what the future might hold with advanced Dyson Sphere technologies, we must also consider the role of cultural preservation. The narrative surrounding technological progress can sometimes overshadow the importance of cultural identities, but as we merge our societies toward the cosmos, it is imperative that we honor the traditions, values, and histories of all engaged communities. Fostering cultural resilience amidst advancements ensures that technological balance is framed not only by efficiency but by deep respect for the intricate tapestries of life that define diverse civilizations.

Furthermore, ethical vigilance must underpin our pursuits as we engage with Dyson Sphere technologies. The ability to manipulate stellar energy introduces a profound level of responsibility, compelling us to establish ethical guidelines that govern our relationship with nature and life itself. Just as we strive to achieve greatness, we must remain cognizant of the moral implications surrounding our technological choices—the potential consequences that wielding such power might have on the broader cosmic community.

In summary, the quests for technological balance in the context of Dyson Sphere constructions embody the need for advanced civilizations to reflect on their values, principles, and responsibilities. Engaging in sustainable practices, promoting equity, celebrating cultural diversity, and establishing ethical frameworks will forge a path toward a future characterized by cooperation and admiration for the intricate relationships that bind us to all life forms. As we endeavor to reach the stars, let us strive to resonate with the delicate harmonies of existence, embracing the shared narrative that reflects our collective aspirations and responsibilities among the vast cosmos.

13. Imagining the Future: Scenarios and Hypotheticals

13.1. Pathways of Evolution for Humanity

The concept of humanity's pathways of evolution hinges on our capacity to adapt, innovate, and harmonize with the universe's vast complexities. As we embark on our theoretical journey toward constructing a Dyson Sphere, a monumental construct that could harness the energy of an entire star, we must consider how this endeavor may catalyze profound cultural and technological evolutions within humanity.

Firstly, the sheer ambition required to create a Dyson Sphere would necessitate a paradigm shift in how societies engage with technology. It may inspire future generations to cultivate a collective mentality that prioritizes collaboration and shared goals. This shift could foster intercontinental partnerships that transcend geographical and cultural boundaries, aligning efforts toward a common purpose—mastering stellar energy extraction. Citizens, scientists, and engineers united by a singular vision of energy harnessing could lead to an era defined by mutual support in innovation and exploration.

Furthermore, as humanity acquires the ability to capture and utilize immense energy resources, new paradigms may emerge regarding resource allocation and sustainability practices. As societies adapt to the value of abundant energy, we might witness the dismantling of outdated paradigms grounded in scarcity. Instead, educational frameworks rooted in sustainability could proliferate, equipping future generations with the knowledge and ethical perspectives required to wisely manage planetary ecosystems while exploring life beyond our home.

The technological advancements achieved through Dyson Sphere initiatives could also foster new industries focused on cosmic engineering, energy management, and ecological preservation. The transformative powers of such initiatives would not only create jobs but also redefine how humanity perceives work and purpose amidst the cosmic tapestry. Fields like materials science, systems engineering, and astrophysics would likely witness unprecedented growth as researchers push the boundaries of exploration and innovation, sparking creative energy among diverse disciplines.

Additionally, the cultural reflections arising from these developments could catalyze new art forms, philosophical inquiries, and identity constructions. Artists may delve into the aesthetics of cosmic energy and its ecological ramifications, bridging the gap between technology and creativity. Literary narratives may evolve to explore themes of harmony between civilizations engaging with stellar energies, encouraging dialogue on ethics, responsibility, and interconnectedness in a broader cosmic context. The burgeoning narratives of Dyson Sphere technology would thus cultivate a cultural renaissance, inviting humanity to celebrate not only advancement but the rich experiences and values that define us.

Moreover, the pathways of evolution may also lead humanity to grapple with complex existential questions. As we harness the power of stars, society will inevitably confront notions of identity and belonging amid an expanding cosmic community. The potential for contact with other intelligent civilizations raises paradigmatic queries: what does it mean to be human when we transcend our terrestrial confines? How can we embrace diversity while pursuing the knowledge and shared experiences that bind our existence to the broader universe?

In considering the implications of Dyson Sphere development, ethical dimensions rise to the forefront, urging society to uphold values that reflect respect, equity, and sustainability. The evolution of governance structures may pivot towards more egalitarian models that prioritize collective decision-making, ensuring the equitable distribution of resources across civilizations and within communities.

In summary, the pathways of evolution for humanity in the context of Dyson Sphere initiatives could signify a transformative journey shaped by collaboration, innovation, and profound cultural introspection. As we navigate the complexities of energy harvesting from stars, we ground our aspirations in ethical consideration and sustainable practices that honor the multifaceted tapestry of existence. In doing so, we empower future generations to cultivate a legacy wherein humanity stands not just as conquerors of the cosmos but as custodians, nurturers, and integral participants within the vast and wondrous universe.

13.2. Potential Discoveries and Their Societal Impact

The potential discoveries arising from the ambitious endeavor of constructing Dyson Spheres would resonate deeply with humanity's quest for knowledge, innovation, and connection. As civilizations strive to harness the energy of stars, the implications of such technological feats could influence diverse areas encompassing culture, economics, governance, and ethics. Exploring these discoveries compels a critical examination of how they might reshape society, provide new pathways for collaboration, and amplify our collective understanding of life in the cosmos.

At the heart of the transformative potential of Dyson Sphere technologies rests the abundance of energy they could generate. Should a civilization successfully construct such a megastructure, it would unlock access to a virtually limitless energy source, fundamentally altering resource management dynamics. This energy abundance could lead to the development of entirely new industries focused on energy storage, transportation, and utilization, sparking economic growth. The shift from energy scarcity to abundance would allow societies to invest in innovative projects that address pressing issues such as climate change, poverty alleviation, and interstellar exploration. Suddenly, the very limitations that bound human potential could dissolve, inviting new horizons filled with possibilities.

Furthermore, the societal impacts of this energy revolution would ripple through governance structures as well. Entities within a Dyson Sphere's purview might prioritize redistributive policies that ensure equitable access to energy resources across communities. The ability to allocate vast quantities of energy efficiently could pave the way for unprecedented levels of collective well-being, as energy becomes a common resource fueling technological innovations and societal advancements. This could mark a significant shift in how power dynamics are structured in human society, fostering collaborative governance models that rely on transparency, inclusivity, and shared responsibilities.

The interplay between energy availability and creative expression cannot be overstated. Cultural narratives surrounding Dyson Spheres may inspire a reimagining of art, literature, and philosophy as societies explore themes of responsibility, sustainability, and interconnectedness. As the quest for energy and technological advances unfolds, artistic expressions may mirror these aspirations, weaving intricate tales that reflect both the glory and the challenges of navigating a new era. The celebration of human creativity, alongside scientific achievement, will play an essential role in shaping identity and cultural cohesion in societies empowered by Dyson Sphere technologies.

In addition, the discoveries surrounding Dyson Sphere technology could catalyze dialogues focused on extraterrestrial life and the ethical responsibilities that accompany our expanding reach into the cosmos. If humanity were to encounter advanced civilizations capable of executing similar feats of engineering, these interactions would demand careful consideration of ethical engagement, shared values, and cultural sensitivity. As we probe the fabric of cosmic existence, the potential for meaningful exchanges of knowledge and ideas becomes apparent—illuminating the importance of fostering a galactic community based on mutual understanding and empathy.

Moreover, the societal impact of potential discoveries extends into the realm of philosophy and existential inquiry. The autonomy granted to civilizations through access to abundant energy invites deeper reflections on the nature of life and our place in the cosmos. With the ability to manipulate cosmic forces comes the responsibility to consider how these advancements align with ethical considerations

—urging societies to continuously examine the implications of their choices on both local and universal scales.

In summary, the potential discoveries arising from Dyson Sphere endeavors could revolutionize human society in multifaceted ways. The availability of vast energy resources has the power to redefine governance structures, spark economic growth, inform cultural narratives, and catalyze ethical dialogues with extraterrestrial civilizations. As we embrace the opportunities and challenges present within these transformative journeys, we must navigate our path with a commitment to equity, sustainability, and responsibility—ensuring that our cosmic aspirations resonate with a recognition of the delicate threads that bind all life in the universe.

Imagining a future civilization shaped by the technological advances and expressions of Dyson Sphere construction compels us to explore how these structures could fundamentally alter societal dynamics, cultural narratives, and human aspirations. As we gaze into the possibilities that lie ahead, we are invited to envision the profound implications of harnessing stellar energy on a cosmic scale, reflecting on how these ambitions might inform our journeys as explorers and stewards of life.

Across the narratives surrounding Dyson Sphere technologies, we encounter the potential for profound societal evolution. The quest for energy abound propels civilizations to prioritize collaborative frameworks, allowing for the fostering of intercontinental partnerships aimed at optimizing resource utilization. The possibility of transitioning from scarcity-driven competition to cooperation highlights a collective mindset that intertwines social responsibility with technological ambition.

In this imagined future, the abundance of stellar energy harvested through Dyson Spheres could revolutionize economies, enabling societies to engage in sustainable practices that prioritize ecological integrity and equitable access to resources. The emergence of innovative industries rooted in energy management encourages a seismic shift in how communities approach knowledge sharing and technological development. Society's values may evolve to prioritize inclusivity, collaboration, and shared aspirations as pivotal elements of progress.

Furthermore, the cultural landscape within this future civilization could experience revitalization as artistic expressions burgeon in response to technological advancements inspired by Dyson Sphere projects. The narratives woven into music, literature, and art would reflect the themes of interconnectedness and responsibility arising from humanity's commitment to harnessing cosmic resources sustainably. The stories crafted in this era may serve as mirrors, amplifying voices that celebrate diversity and recognize our intertwined fates as custodians of life across the cosmos.

However, as we envision these advancements, we must also grapple with the ethical considerations tied to interstellar engagement. The presence of Dyson Spheres signifies humanity's potential to reach beyond its terrestrial confines, but with it arises the moral imperative to navigate relationships with other intelligent civilizations with respect and humility. The interactions we cultivate with these advanced societies must be built within frameworks that honor distinct cultural identities and prioritize ethical stewardship over mere technological progress.

In conclusion, the future civilization shaped by the realization of Dyson Sphere technologies invites reflections on societal evolution, cultural expression, and ethical engagement. As we pursue our ambitions to harness stellar energy, we are positioned to create a narrative emanating from cooperation, sustainability, and mutual respect. A legacy founded on these principles ensures that our journey to the stars is not defined solely by technological achievements but reflects the values that unite us as a shared cosmic community.

As we consider the potential impacts of Dyson Sphere constructions on our solar system, we embark on an investigative journey that probes the intricate relationships between advanced engineering and celestial dynamics. The construction of colossal megastructures capable of harnessing stellar energy presents both unprecedented opportunities and formidable challenges—prompting us to reflect on the immediate and far-reaching consequences of these endeavors on our solar neighborhood.

The impact of a Dyson Sphere on the solar system encompasses profound transformations across multiple dimensions. First and foremost, the energy dynamics surrounding a star would experience significant alterations as a consequence of capturing and utilizing stellar output. The energy harvesting activities may lead to deviations in solar radiation patterns for neighboring planets and moons, potentially affecting their climates, ecosystems, and habitability. Should energy collection take the form of a rigid structure, the interplay between the star and its celestial neighbors may provoke cascading effects, altering the equilibrium that supports life in these environments.

Consider the implications of gravitational interactions that arise from constructing such immense structures. The Dyson Sphere, whether envisioned as a solid shell or a dispersed array of components, would exert gravitational forces on nearby celestial bodies—altering orbits and potentially destabilizing established planetary dynamics. Communities residing on planets within these systems, contemplating their futures, would need to prepare for changes in the gravitational forces governing their environments, echoing throughout ecosystems and impacting the very fabric of life.

Moreover, as Dyson Sphere technologies facilitate unprecedented resource mobilization and logistics within the solar system, we must consider the ecological aspects tied to extraction practices. The potential for harvesting materials from asteroids, moons, or other celestial bodies amplifies our responsibilities as stewards of extraterrestrial environments. It becomes imperative to ensure that resource acquisition practices prioritize sustainability and ecological preservation, safeguarding the delicate balances that sustain life in neighboring worlds.

In addition to the immediate repercussions sowed throughout the solar system, the societal ramifications of Dyson Sphere construction extend into our narrative as inhabitants of Earth. The introduction of abundant energy resources could catalyze a shift in social structures—tackling longstanding issues of energy access, poverty, and resource scarcity. New models of collaboration may arise as communities unite around energy-rich futures, fostering a culture rooted in cooperation and sustainability.

Furthermore, as we advance technologically and expand our reach into the cosmos, the ethical implications of our actions become paramount. Each decision made in the context of constructing a Dyson Sphere must reflect a commitment to ensuring that both present and future generations benefit from the energy derived from stellar sources. Perspectives grounded in environmental ethics will shape the frameworks guiding our interactions with celestial bodies and the choices made regarding their resources.

In conclusion, the potential impacts of Dyson Sphere constructions manifest as complex layers of transformation within our solar system. From energy dynamics and gravitational interactions to ecological preservation and societal evolution, the implications unfold a narrative rich in responsibility and reflection. As we continue this journey of exploration, let us ensure that our endeavors resonate with values of sustainability, stewardship, and ethical engagement, guiding us toward a future defined by harmony among all forms of life across the cosmos.

As we delve into the imaginative landscape of alternative futures enabled by megaengineering ventures like Dyson Spheres, we open a portal to a wealth of possibilities that transgress the limits of our current aspirations. The charting of new pathways presents numerous scenarios that illuminate humanity's potential trajectories as society engages with advanced technologies capable of harnessing stellar energy.

One prospective future may embody a utopian vision—one in which the allure of abundant energy unlocks unprecedented opportunities for growth, exploration, and collaboration among diverse civilizations. As societies acquire the means to capture stellar energy, the constraints of energy scarcity dissolve, liberating human creativity and innovation. A culture flourishing in energy abundance could redirect its focus from survival toward imaginative pursuits, fostering an environment conducive to artistic expression, scientific advancement, and sustainable practices.

In this context, the societal implications of Dyson Sphere technologies may also provoke reconceptualizations of governance structures and social frameworks. Empowered by energy independence, communities may prioritize collective well-being over individual ambition —cultivating systems that emphasize equity, collaboration, and participatory decision-making. This transformation could herald an era marked by transparency, resilience, and harmony as societies engage meaningfully with the ecological landscapes they inhabit.

Conversely, alternate future scenarios may evoke cautionary tales —visibly depicting the consequences of overreach, inequity, or exploitation driven by the allure of vast energy resources. The race to construct Dyson Spheres may lead to significant disparities among civilizations, leaving less advanced societies vulnerable to being overshadowed or dominated. In such a narrative, the lessons gleaned from history echo—highlighting the complexities of oppression, ecological degradation, and the rise of authoritarianism in the face of tremendous power.

These narratives compel societies to remain vigilant, ensuring that pursuits of cosmic ambition are accompanied by deep ethical reflections and considerations of communal welfare. The rise of a dystopian reality presents an opportunity to embrace sustainable practices and equitable resource allocation as necessary pillars for advancing technology. By weaving together values of cooperation, respect, and ecological preservation, a future characterized by Dyson Sphere technologies could avoid the pitfalls of exploitative governance.

Moreover, envisioning the future pathways of Dyson Sphere technologies invites us to explore the emergence of collaborative cosmic economies. As civilizations venture into the business of harnessing star energy, these opportunities could cultivate partnerships that transcend borders and promote interstellar cooperation. The potential for trade in energy, knowledge, and technology may give rise to new forms of galactic governance—crystallizing an interconnected tapestry woven from shared values, lessons learned, and collaborative aspirations.

In summary, the imaginative exploration of alternative futures enabled by Dyson Sphere technologies leads us to understand that our aspirations can give rise to both utopian possibilities and dystopian challenges. The trajectories we chart in our embrace of cosmic energy remind us of our responsibilities as stewards of the universe, urging us to align our technological ambitions with ethical considerations that prioritize sustainability, equity, and mutual respect. As we navigate the intricate pathways ahead, we reinforce the narrative that our journey among the stars is marked by choices that reflect the best of our humanity—creating a legacy that resonates throughout the cosmos.

As we envision the technological futures grounded in Dyson Sphere initiatives, we must also navigate the intricate pathways of ambition, responsibility, and ethical exploration. Each potential reality brought forth by megaengineering ventures invites us to reflect on our roles as cosmic stewards, prompting profound inquiries about the implications of wielding such monumental power.

The advancements facilitated by Dyson Spheres would undoubtedly lead to energy-rich societies capable of shaping their futures. However, along with the prospect of abundance lies the responsibility to acknowledge and address the complexities associated with wielding colossal energies harnessed from stellar sources. The moral obligation to approach energy management with foresight and equity becomes paramount as we navigate the implications of these technologies and the vast cosmic systems that intersect with them.

Envisioned futures may reflect societies that embrace sustainability through responsible use of energy resources and proactive management of ecological principles. The lessons garnered through the ongoing construction and operation of Dyson Spheres could prompt a shift away from systems dependent on fossil fuels or resource exploitation, guiding a transition toward ecological stewardship and conservation within diverse environments. Imagined communities may find inspiration in principles that prioritize the well-being of all life forms—where collective energy management fosters a culture of cooperation, empathy, and interdependence.

The complexities of interstellar interactions will require vigilance as communities engage with advanced civilizations, ensuring that ethical considerations guide decision-making processes in resource allocation, technology sharing, and ecological preservation. As the potential for collaboration across galaxies unfolds, the importance of establishing frameworks that promote understanding, respect, and equity cannot be overstated.

Moreover, the pursuit of Dyson Spheres can catalyze a cultural renaissance—one that celebrates artistic expression, scientific inquiry, and philosophical reflection. As societies grapple with the challenges presented by advanced technologies, the exploration of new narratives born from our cosmic ambitions invites us to explore the intersections of life and technology, creativity and ethics. Artists, scientists, and thinkers will embody the multidimensional tapestry of existence as they reflect upon our aspirations among the stars.

Ultimately, the technological futures forged through Dyson Sphere projects will define humanity's trajectory in the universe—a narrative woven from values of balance, sustainability, and shared aspirations. As we traverse new pathways toward cosmic exploration, we reaffirm our commitment to enrich the human experience, embodying the qualities that unite us as sentient beings reaching for the stars. With each step into the vast unknown, let us continue to pursue a legacy marked by accountability and hope, fostering harmonious existence within the intricate tapestry of cosmic life.

13.3. Imagining a Future Civilization

Imagining a future civilization where Dyson Spheres are not merely theoretical constructs but tangible realities invites profound reflections on the transformative potential of humanity's technological pursuits. In this landscape, we find ourselves contemplating the societal, cultural, and ethical implications of harnessing stellar energy, fundamentally redefining what it means to be a civilization among the stars.

Firstly, the realization of Dyson Sphere technologies could catalyze a seismic shift in resource management and energy consumption. Energy abundance would eliminate the competing interests traditionally associated with terrestrial energy resources, encouraging a collaborative mindset rooted in sustainability. As energy from stars becomes readily available, societies may shift from zero-sum ideologies that pit scarcity against survival to frameworks emphasizing shared growth and community well-being. This transition would pave the way for innovations that prioritize ecological integrity while redirecting focus toward enhanced quality of life, exploration, and creativity.

Moreover, as advanced civilizations engage in constructing Dyson Spheres, education and innovation would likely flourish. The pursuit of energy harvesting technologies opens doors for interdisciplinary research, fostering collaborations between scientists, engineers, artists, and ethicists. As humanity integrates knowledge from various domains, new educational paradigms may emerge that celebrate inquiry, adaptability, and creativity. The emphasis on holistic and sustainable approaches to problem-solving could facilitate a future where conflict resolution and cooperation characterize societal interactions among diverse cultures.

Equally important, the cultural landscape shaped by Dyson Sphere technologies will be marked by a resurgence of artistic expression, philosophical inquiry, and narrative exploration. Artistic endeavors inspired by the vastness of the cosmos, the beauty of harmonic existence, and the challenges of ethical engagement may proliferate, fostering a cultural renaissance that echoes the aspirations of communities reaching for the stars. These artistic expressions could serve as vessels for articulating the dreams, fears, and interconnectedness of all life—a celebration of the complexities and wonders of existence.

In contemplating the implications of a future civilization enabled by Dyson Sphere technologies, we must grapple with the ethical responsibilities that come with cosmic ambitions. The power to harness stellar energy means engaging in continual reflection regarding ecological stewardship, interstellar cooperation, and the well-being of all life forms we may encounter. As these civilizations become custodians of stellar energy, their ethical frameworks—informed by past experiences, cultural values, and the desire for equity—will shape their approach to encounters with potential extraterrestrial life.

Furthermore, envisioning a future intertwined with Dyson Sphere technologies invites discussions about social equity and governance. With immense energy resources at their disposal, advanced civilizations must prioritize inclusive decision-making processes that ensure fair resource allocation. By embedding principles of transparency and communal participation into their governance structures, societies can maintain a commitment to justice and foster resilience against inequalities that could arise in the face of such abundance.

However, as we explore such possibilities, the challenges inevitably interwoven with ambitious technological undertakings must not be dismissed. The narratives surrounding Dyson Spheres compel a commitment to ecological responsibility as civilizations grapple with the implications of energy consumption on their environments and the potential consequences that arise from resource extraction across celestial bodies. Balancing ambition with respect for the delicate nuances of ecosystems will be vital to ensuring the long-term sustainability of advanced civilizations.

In summary, the imagination of a future civilization shaped by Dyson Sphere technologies presents a tapestry rich in potential and complexity. As societies harness the energy of stars, we are invited to explore themes of sustainability, ethical engagement, and cultural evolution. The implications for interstellar cooperation, artistic expression, and inclusive governance resonate throughout our discourse, urging us to cultivate a legacy characterized by compassion, creativity, and commitment to balanced growth amidst the vast cosmic tapestry. As we envision our role as builders of the future, the aspiration to reach the stars becomes entwined with the profound responsibilities of being stewards of life and knowledge across the universe.

The potential impacts a Dyson Sphere may impart on our solar system are straddled between transformative advancements and complex dynamism demanding nuanced reflection. Constructing such colossal engineering marvels signifies humanity's drive to overcome energy constraints, yet the consequences of these undertakings envelop the celestial ecosystem within which we reside, calling for careful consideration and proactive stewardship.

Imagining the far-reaching implications, the first consideration centers on the immediate environmental dynamics occurring once a Dyson Sphere is erected. Surrounding a star with an energy-collecting structure would alter the balance of solar energy distribution across neighboring planets and moons. Fluctuations in energy transport could significantly impact climatic conditions and ecological systems, possibly introducing shifts in planet-wide temperatures and weather patterns dependent on stellar radiation. The ecological consequences may ripple through existing biospheres, inherently reshaping the trajectories of evolution and sustainability for life forms residing on these celestial bodies.

Alongside these immediate shifts emerges a critical conversation on resource acquisition leading up to and during the construction of a Dyson Sphere. The demand for raw materials beyond Earth necessitates widespread mining endeavors targeting celestial bodies such as asteroids, moons, or even other planets. Weighing the implications of resource extraction against the conservation of planets and their ecosystems becomes paramount, ensuring that our quest for energy does not take a toll on the intrinsic value of life throughout the solar system. This extended ecological discourse emphasizes the importance of incorporating ethical practices within our interstellar engagements, framing resource management strategies that respect the interconnectedness of all life.

Moreover, the gravitational dynamics within the solar system pose significant challenges when operating a Dyson Sphere. The magnitude of such structures inherently alters gravitational interactions, potentially destabilizing planetary orbits or affecting the trajectories of smaller celestial bodies. The introduction of new gravitational variables calls for meticulous monitoring and adjustment to safeguard the balance necessary for a sustainable cosmic landscape. The delicate dance of celestial mechanics will demand precise calculations and ongoing engagement with the dynamics of the solar system as societies strive to maintain stability amidst immense energy harvesting endeavors.

Additionally, as civilizations are propelled into a future shaped by Dyson Sphere technologies, societal implications begin to unfold. The transition from energy scarcity to an age of energy abundance presents significant opportunities—broadening the scope for exploration, creativity, and innovation. Consideration of educational frameworks, cultural shifts, and social structures will become fundamental as advanced civilizations redefine their interactions with energy resources and each other.

As we navigate through the ramifications of Dyson Spheres on the solar system, we invite deeper contemplation of our responsibilities as cosmic citizens. Ensuring that our actions resonate with principles of equity and environmental integrity will define how we approach the vast energies that await our harnessing. Through deliberate stewardship and ethical reflection, we can embark on this extraordinary journey, not merely as conquerors of energy but as nurturers of the delicate balance of life that perpetuates throughout the celestial realm.

In summary, the potential impacts of Dyson Sphere constructions within our solar system invite intricate discussions on ecological, gravitational, and societal dynamics. As we explore the ramifications of these monumental undertakings, we must embrace a cultural commitment to sustainability and ethical responsibility, ensuring our cosmic aspirations align with values that honor the richness of existence across all celestial bodies. Through our journeys among the stars, we affirm our role as custodians of energy, knowledge, and life —crafting a legacy that resonates throughout the cosmos.

Imagining alternative futures constructed from the threads of Dyson Sphere technologies presents serendipitous opportunities for deep exploration into new societal configurations, cultural narratives, and ethical considerations. As we vividly envision the possibilities and challenges associated with cosmic energy harvesting, the path forward evokes diverse scenarios—ranging from utopian optimism to cautionary tales of exploitation and environmental degradation.

At the heart of the alternative futures inspired by Dyson Sphere technologies is the notion that energy abundance could cultivate transformative societal evolution. By embracing shared technologies that harvest stellar energies, humanity may transcend resource scarcity, ushering in a cultural renaissance characterized by seamless interconnections, innovation, and integration of diverse industries. The paradigm shift could redefine our civic responsibilities as cultures meld harmoniously around shared objectives—emphasizing community well-being and ecological stewardship, ultimately nurturing a more collaborative spirit in a previously fragmented world.

However, woven through these optimistic narratives lurks the importance of caution and vigilance. The allure of limitless energy bears the risk of fostering inequities and power imbalances that have historically shaped human societies. In scenarios where Dyson Sphere constructs become symbols of prosperity, the opportunity for exploitation may escalate, leaving marginalized groups vulnerable to the repercussions of advanced technologies. Addressing these risks calls for collective ethical considerations grounded in values of equity, justice, and inclusivity—a reflective discourse that promotes the harmonization of opportunities across diverse populations during a transformational period.

Moreover, the exploration of potential discoveries resulting from Dyson Sphere endeavors further embodies the rich complexities that await us. Uncovering remnants of advanced civilizations wielding similar structures may inspire profound insights into technological trajectories while instigating questions about identity and cultural significance. As humanity engages with the legacy of others in the cosmos, the narratives surrounding Dyson Sphere technologies may serve to enrich or complicate our understanding of life across celestial environments.

Contemplating these alternative futures invites us to critically examine the narratives we construct and enforce as we illuminate our path toward cosmic energy harvesting. The pursuit of Dyson Sphere technologies becomes a mirror that challenges us to reflect on our commitments to sustainability and social equity. In doing so, we ensure that our cosmic ambitions, informed by ethical principles, are not merely technological achievements but resonate with a sense of purpose that celebrates interconnection—both among civilizations on Earth and with those we may encounter beyond our solar system.

In closing, the exploration of alternative futures shaped by Dyson Sphere initiatives unveils the exciting potential for advancement while underscoring the responsibilities we hold as stewards of our technological legacy. Embracing inclusive narratives that reflect cooperation, sustainability, and equity will not only guide societies through this transformative journey but also enrich the tapestry of existence we share with the cosmos. As we reach for the stars, let our aspirations be tempered by humility and reflection, ensuring our journey leaves a positive mark on the universes we access.

13.4. Impacts on the Solar System

As we delve into the potential impacts on the solar system stemming from the construction and operation of a Dyson Sphere, it is crucial to engage in a comprehensive analysis of the myriad ways such an extraordinary engineering feat could reshape our celestial environment. The Dyson Sphere, an immense structure capable of harvesting the energy produced by a star, transcends mere speculation to evoke profound implications for planetary dynamics, ecological systems, and interstellar relations. This exploration invites us to consider both immediate and far-reaching consequences of such monumental undertakings.

To begin with, one of the most significant impacts of constructing a Dyson Sphere on a star like our sun would be the modification of energy distribution within the solar system. By harnessing the vast energy output of the sun, the direct light and heat available to nearby planets—such as Earth, Mars, and even distant realms like Saturn and Jupiter—could be dramatically altered. This alteration may lead to multifaceted changes in climatic conditions, environmental patterns, and the viability of life on these celestial bodies.

For instance, energy harvesters around the sun would inevitably reduce the amount of solar radiation reaching planets within the system. Shade provided by the structure could create unique microclimates, potentially rendering certain areas less hospitable or, conversely, creating opportunities for growth in regions that were previously inhospitable. The ecological consequences of these changes would be profound; flora and fauna may need to adapt to improved conditions or confront challenges that arise from fluctuating energy supplies. Questions surrounding climate stability and the adaptability of life forms would demand continued investigation and monitoring.

Furthermore, the construction of a Dyson Sphere would introduce substantial gravitational changes in the solar system. As the structure itself requires a significant mass, these alterations could affect the orbits of planets and other celestial bodies within the solar system. The mechanics of the solar system, which has been finely balanced for billions of years, could be destabilized as the gravitational influence of the Dyson Sphere shifts the positions of planets, moons, and asteroids. This raises substantial questions regarding how these gravitational shifts might affect existing equilibria and whether they could lead to unforeseen collisions or orbital instabilities.

Equally important is the ecological responsibility that accompanies the construction and operation of Dyson Sphere technology. The alluring prospect of harnessing a star's energy imposes obligations on aspiring civilizations to consider the ecological footprint of their efforts. As materials are extracted from asteroids and other celestial bodies for the construction of the Dyson Sphere, the potential impact on local ecosystems and planetary balances must be addressed. Therefore, adopting sustainable practices to preserve the integrity of planetary environments becomes essential in the pursuit of stellar energy harnessing.

Moreover, the emergence of Dyson Sphere technologies would likely prompt reevaluations of social structures within the solar system. The transition from energy scarcity to abundance could transform economic systems and societal dynamics, potentially leading to new power balances among different planetary settlements. Civilizations could establish governance structures focused on equitable distribution of resources, emphasizing cooperation and collective decision-making while reimagining relationships between citizens of different planets.

As we consider the vast implications of constructing a Dyson Sphere on our solar system, we must remain vigilant about the ethical dimensions surrounding these technologies. Engaging with other intelligent civilizations capable of similar advancements urges us to reflect on how we navigate interstellar relations. The ethics of stewardship, knowledge sharing, and the treatment of other life forms must guide our pursuits, ensuring that our cosmic ambitions reflect respect and responsibility.

In conclusion, the potential impacts of Dyson Sphere constructions on our solar system illustrate a delicate interplay of ecological, gravitational, and societal dynamics. As we venture into the realm of cosmic energy harvesting, we must commit to ensuring our actions resonate with values of sustainability, equity, and respect for the complexities of life throughout the universe. By embracing these principles, humanity can harness the transformative power of Dyson Spheres while nurturing a harmonious relationship with the celestial environments that endure alongside our expansion among the stars.

Imagining alternative futures constructed around the realization of Dyson Sphere technologies beckons us to explore the depth of possibilities that transcend our current realities and illuminate new paths for navigating societal dynamics, cultural shifts, and ethical considerations. As we gaze into the potentials presented by colossal engineering efforts, we discover narratives rich with opportunities that may redefine the trajectory of civilization.

One promising future may herald a generative landscape characterized by energy abundance, transforming how societies engage with resources and sustainability. In this paradigm, the allure of plentiful energy harvested from stars could facilitate the development of futuristic cities that prioritize well-being, ecological preservation, and shared governance. Rather than withering under the constraints posed by energy scarcity, communities may thrive as abundant energy enables innovation, creativity, and exploration.

With the increased availability of energy, educational frameworks would likely be transformed to inspire interdisciplinary learning that embraces collaboration and problem-solving across diverse fields. A culture of curiosity and exploration may blossom, where tomorrow's leaders are trained not just to navigate traditional disciplines but to engage with the tech-savvy, globally-minded citizens of an energy-rich future—embarking on inquiries into the cosmos while continually reflecting on their ethical responsibilities towards others.

However, the visions of abundance must not obscure the potential for dystopian narratives to emerge alongside societal advancements. As desirous as these futures may seem, the responsibility to prevent inequalities from surfacing looms large. The prospect of Dyson Sphere technology may give rise to significant disparities among civilizations capable of harnessing stellar energy as resource exploitation brings forth old patterns of dominance. This cautionary tale urges societies to prioritize equity, environmental stewardship, and collective well-being—ensuring that the benefits brought by such technologies are shared widely and not concentrated in a privileged few.

Additionally, envisioning alternative futures raises questions about our interstellar identity and relationship with extraterrestrial civilizations. As we consider the potential for encountering other intelligent societies, reflections on shared values, cultural preservation, and ethical engagement to uphold dignity and mutual respect become vital. A future evolved through Dyson Sphere energy may ultimately necessitate a broader understanding of cosmic citizenship—one that recognizes the interdependence of various life forms within the vast tapestry of existence.

Furthermore, the cultural and artistic landscapes within these alternative futures are likely to flourish as creativity dances alongside scientific progression. Narratives surrounding Dyson Sphere technologies would inspire poetic expressions, visual art, and lyrical compositions that celebrate cosmic exploration and interplanetary connections. The narratives we craft in this renaissance—a fusion of artistry and science—serve not only as reflections of values but as emotional conduits that unite societies across stellar distances.

In summary, the exploration of alternative futures constructed through Dyson Sphere technologies invites a rich tapestry of possibilities for collective evolution. From energy abundance to ethical engagements, our narratives illuminate the depth of human imagination and the responsibilities we carry. Embracing cooperation, sustainability, and equity will be essential as we forge a path through the stars—ensuring that our legacy resonates powerfully across the cosmos, embodying the aspirations and identities of life throughout the journey.

As we engage with the larger implications of creating Dyson Spheres, we find ourselves embarking on a journey of transformational change

—one marked by the potential to redefine energy dynamics, societal structures, and cultural narratives. These constructions invite us to imagine new realities and possibilities that merge technological prowess with ethical commitment, catapulting us into futures previously unfathomable.

Contemplating the societal transformations brought about by Dyson Sphere technologies, we are prompted to reflect on how abundance alters the fabric of communities. The transition from scarcity could dissolve traditional power hierarchies, giving rise to a more inclusive governance framework rooted in cooperation and collective decision-making. As energy becomes readily available, societies may prioritize community well-being and sustainability through shared governance models that encourage collaboration across diverse populations.

Furthermore, this shift may inspire a cultural renaissance characterized by creativity and innovation. As societies embark on their quests to construct Dyson Spheres, they could ignite vibrant artistic expressions that celebrate the Webs of connection that unite life across the cosmos. Music, literature, and visual arts may evoke themes of exploration and interdependence, amplifying humanity's aspirations and reminding us of the beauty inherent in collaboration.

However, navigating this transformative landscape also requires grappling with the potential consequences of energy abundance. The allure of Dyson Sphere technologies carry risks of exploitation, inequities, and ecological degradation. Caution must guide decision-makers as they pursue advancements that carry broad implications for the environment and society. Communities must strive to establish equitable frameworks that ensure access to resources is shared among all—guarding against the chance of new forms of social stratification manifesting as the consequence of energy harvest.

Additionally, in this imagined future lies the possibility of cultural encounters with advanced civilizations. Contact with intelligent life capable of constructing Dyson Spheres would not only excite curiosity but also prompt reflection on our responsibilities as interstellar citizens. Honest dialogues, premised on mutual respect and understanding, become quintessential as we navigate the complexities of shared spaces, ensuring that our interactions reflect our commitment to equity and cooperation.

In summary, the implications of Dyson Sphere technologies on society urge us to embrace transformation with a focus on ethical governance and cultural collaboration. As we journey through the cosmos, let us carry forth the spirit of inclusivity that binds us, ensuring our pursuits reflect the very essence of our shared humanity. The legacy we craft in this new era will resonate far beyond our solar system—poised to unfold beautifully across the infinite tapestry of existence as we chart paths to galaxies unknown.

Envisioning a world rooted in technological balance and sustainability, we find threads connecting our cosmic pursuits with the very essence of our humanity. As we stand on the threshold of the extraordinary, engaged in the monumental task of harnessing celestial energies, we must navigate pathways that embrace both ambition and ethical responsibility—allowing us to collectively shape the narratives that define life throughout the cosmos.

Imagining the future involves recognizing the intricate dance between ambition and stewardship; as we pursue Dyson Sphere technologies in our quest for energy, we embody the profound responsibility that accompanies such power. By fostering technologies that harmonize with the ecological landscapes from which they arise, we create a collaborative interplay that elevates both humanity and nature.

The journey toward a future characterized by Dyson Sphere technologies also facilitates dialogues surrounding resource management and community engagement, empowering societies to embrace inclusive decision-making structures. As the aspirations for interstellar energy harvesting become realities, our collective understanding of equity emerges, fostering a culture anchored in mutual respect for diverse identities across the cosmos. Engagement in this cultural and ethical renaissance invites us to expand our definitions of community—recognizing the interconnectedness we share with all life forms.

Moreover, as we gaze into the boundless possibilities presented by Dyson Sphere initiatives, we are reminded of the artistic and philosophical dimensions that resonate within our ambitions. The cosmic energy harnessed from stars may ignite a cultural renaissance, at once reflective of society's experiences and aspirations. Artistic expressions could flourish, encompassing the themes of exploration and cooperation. Weaving these narratives into the very fabric of our aspirations, we can inspire future generations to envision their own contributions to the ever-evolving tapestry of cosmic identity.

In conclusion, the interplay of aspirations surrounding Dyson Sphere technologies invites us to imagine a future fluently engaged with principles of sustainability, cooperation, and collective well-being. By anchoring these pursuits in ethical responsibility, we pave paths that echo through the cosmos—creating a legacy defined by harmony, technological balance, and recognition of the threads that connect us all. As we embark on this journey beyond our terrestrial confines, let our narrative resonate with a commitment to embrace the shared story of existence amid the stars.

13.5. Alternative Futures for Megaengineering

In considering the future of megaengineering, particularly through the lens of Dyson Sphere technology, we unlock a multitude of divergent pathways that humanity could traverse. Each of these scenarios reflects not only our technological ambitions but also the ethical considerations, societal structures, and ecological responsibilities that accompany such grand endeavors. As we delve into alternative futures, we encounter potential outcomes framed by both optimism and caution, inspiring reflection on how we navigate the complexities surrounding the quest for abundant energy harvested from stars.

One optimistic scenario envisions the emergence of an energy-rich civilization, where the successful construction of Dyson Spheres transforms the dynamics of life on Earth and beyond. The existence of such structures would herald an era characterized by an abundance of energy, which could alleviate resource scarcity and erase long-standing societal inequities. Freed from the burdens of fossil fuel dependence, societies may witness rejuvenation in their cultural, scientific, and artistic expressions as creativity flourishes within a context of infinite resources. Innovations in education, art, and technology could thrive as communities come together to collaborate and explore new frontiers—facilitating rapid advancements in multiple fields.

Additionally, this future civilization may prioritize sustainability and ecological stewardship, actively advocating for a harmonious relationship between technological ambitions and environmental integrity. As Dyson Spheres harvest stellar energy, it is conceivable that societies would employ advanced materials and intelligent systems designed to minimize ecological footprints. This deep-seated commitment to responsible resource management could inspire a cultural renaissance, where concepts of sustainability and stewardship enter the collective consciousness, guiding the ways societies interact with both terrestrial and extraterrestrial ecosystems.

However, in juxtaposition, a more cautionary scenario emerges, warning of the potential pitfalls that accompany the pursuit of megaengineering. The allure of harnessing stellar energy could lead to urges of exploitation, as civilizations prioritize immediate gains over long-term sustainability. If not guided by ethical frameworks promoting equity, the benefits derived from Dyson Spheres may be concentrated among a select few, exacerbating existing disparities and tension between civilizations. Humanity may face a somber reflection on its ability to wield advanced technologies responsibly, invoking echoes of past mistakes associated with colonialism and environmental degradation.

In examining these dark potentials, we are reminded of the complexity inherent in navigating the socio-political dynamics within advanced civilizations. As the power dynamics shift with the introduction of Dyson Sphere technologies, it becomes imperative to foster inclusive governance structures that ensure the equitable distribution of resources and prioritize collective well-being. The formulation of ethical guiding principles for interstellar engagement becomes essential to prevent exploitation or malfeasance among advanced societies, shaping a narrative that embodies collaborative progress rather than conflict.

The notion of interstellar cooperation becomes a vital pillar within these alternative futures. As humanity engages with advanced societies capable of constructing Dyson Spheres, the relational aspects surrounding these encounters may trigger profound philosophical reflections—guiding dialogues that emphasize reciprocity, mutual respect, and cultural preservation. The interactions between disparate civilizations could yield groundbreaking discoveries and innovations, reshaping both societies and our understanding of the cosmos.

Moreover, new opportunities for knowledge exchange may arise as advanced civilizations share insights into sustainable practices around energy management and resource utilization. Engaging in these collaborative initiatives would not only accelerate technological advancement but also cultivate a growing ethos of compassion and understanding that transcends planetary and cultural boundaries.

As we explore the alternative futures arising from Dyson Sphere technologies, we are drawn toward reflections on our own values, ethics, and responsibilities. Each scenario navigates the complexities of ambition, caution, and cooperation—highlighting how we must thread the needle of progress with care and foresight. Understanding that our choices resonate far beyond immediate benefits compels us to adopt a holistic perspective as we strive to harmonize technological advancements with meaningful, sustainable practices that honor the interconnectedness of all life.

In summary, imagining alternative futures stimulated by Dyson Sphere technologies reveals a tapestry of possibilities shaped by both ambitions and responsibilities. The exploration of these scenarios enables humanity to navigate the complexities ahead, forging pathways interwoven with sustainability, equity, and collaborative engagement. As we chart our course among the stars, let us remain mindful that our cosmic journey is not solely defined by technological prowess, but by the richness of our evolving relationships with life—ultimately crafting a legacy reflective of compassion, forward-thinking, and an unwavering commitment to harmonious coexistence amid the cosmos.

www.ingramcontent.com/pod-product-compliance
Lightning Source LLC
Chambersburg PA
CBHW070946050326
40689CB00014B/3359